THE
MOUNTAINEERS

❧

A HISTORY

THE
MOUNTAINEERS

A HISTORY

by

JIM KJELDSEN

KEN LANS
PHOTO EDITOR

THE
MOUNTAINEERS

Published by
The Mountaineers
1001 SW Klickitat Way, Suite 201
Seattle, WA 98134

©1998 by The Mountaineers

First edition, 1998

Published simultaneously in Great Britain by Cordee, 3a DeMontfort Street, Leicester, England, LE1 7HD

Manufactured in the United States of America

Edited by Don Graydon
Cover and book design by Jennifer Shontz
Layout by Jennifer Shontz

*In the captions, an * indicates an individual who is not a member of The Mountaineers*

Cover photograph: *A party studies a giant crevasse at 11,000 feet on Mount Rainier during the 1912 outing.* Photo: H. V. Abel, Special Collections, University of Washington Libraries, neg. no. 18112.
Frontispiece: *On the summit of 9,415-foot Mount Stuart during the 1914 outing: Grace Rand, Eva Macdonald, Mr. and Mrs. H. H. Botten, W. E. Doph, F. Fairbrook, and J. A. Laurie.* Photo: F. Q. Gorton, Special Collections, University of Washington Libraries, neg. no. 14001.

Library of Congress Cataloging-in-Publication Data

Kjeldsen, Jim.
    The Mountaineers: a history / by Jim Kjeldsen: Ken Lans, photo editor.—1st ed.
        p.   cm.
    Includes bibliographical references (p.   ) and index.
    ISBN 0-89886-615-4. —ISBN 0-89886-599-9 (pbk.)
    1. Mountaineers (Society)—History. 2. Mountaineering—Northwest, Pacific—Societies, etc. —History. 3. Outdoor recreation—Northwest, Pacific—Societies, etc. —History. I. Title.
GV191.42.N75K54 1998
796.52'2'060795—dc21   98-7795
                                                   CIP

 Printed on recycled paper

CONTENTS

George MacGowan, Wolf Bauer, Jack Hossack, and Joe Halwax pause to study Mount Goode from its base, planning their route up as they start on their classic first ascent in 1936. Photo: O. P. Dickert

ACKNOWLEDGMENTS

This book is the product of hundreds of hours of effort, most of it by volunteers. Chief among them were author Jim Kjeldsen and photo editor Ken Lans. But many others were also involved, assembling and organizing the information and checking the facts.

The project started in 1992 when Dianne Hoff, then president of The Mountaineers, considered a suggestion by Alexandra Pye and others to form a History Committee, the purpose of which would be to bring together all the historical odds and ends as the club approached its ninetieth year. Hoff recruited Paul Wiseman, a former club president, to be the committee's first chairman. Wiseman in turn enlisted the help of Pye to form a sixteen-person committee.

History Committee members Dianne Hoff, Laura Zalesky, and Bill Zauche recruited researchers and writers from the club's committees. Those researching and writing about historical subjects included Phil Zalesky, conservation efforts; Herb Belanger, climbing; Nedra Slauson, summer outings; Katha Miller-Winder, the Players drama group; Frank Fickeisen, club administration; Neva Karrick, the early days of The Mountaineers Foundation; John Davis, the long search for a clubhouse; Jo Rayl, early skiing; Stella Degenhardt, books publishing; and R. Duke Watson, the part The Mountaineers played in the Army's 10th Mountain Division during World War II.

These reports, together with reports from other committees and branches, and *The Mountaineer* annuals formed the principal sources of information used in compiling this book. Kjeldsen interviewed numerous Mountaineers who had contributed to Northwest climbing history, and Morris Moen, Suzanne Shannon, and others captured the memories of longtime Mountaineers on tape.

Recruited to serve as a Review Subcommittee for this book were History Committee members Laura and Phil Zalesky, Tom Miller, Ken Prestrud, Nedra Slauson, Paul Wiseman, and Bill Zauche. With Laura Zalesky as chair, this group was on call for the entire period of manuscript preparation, meeting to check drafts and pooling their knowledge to ensure accuracy.

As the manuscript began to take shape, Ken Lans conducted an extensive search for photographs, tracking down pictures and methodically identifying people and places. Jim Kurtz and Tom Miller rephotographed many fragile images from early albums for reproduction. Meanwhile, club members donated photos from private collections, and Seattle FilmWorks donated film processing.

Thanks are due for the thoughtful and helpful manuscript reviews by Tom Allen, Alice Bond, Sam Fry, Jim and Nancy Kurtz, Morris Moen, Stan Engle, Paul Robisch, Bill Zauche, John Davis, Max Hollenbeck, Carsten Lien,

Errol Nelson, A. E. Robinson, James Sanford, Norman Winn, Mary Anderson, Steven Cox, Barbara McCann, Mary Fries, Richard Berner, and Dee Molenaar.

The History Committee also wishes to thank Karyl Winn, head of Manuscripts and University Archives, University of Washington Libraries, and the staff of Special Collections for their help in tracking down historical information and for professional advice.

The Mountaineers use a ladder to cross a crevasse on Mount Shuksan during the 1928 outing. Clarence A. "Happy" Fisher had earlier discovered a route (now known as the Fisher Chimneys) up the peak directly across from Lake Ann. Photo: A. H. Hudson, Special Collections, University of Washington Libraries, neg. no. 18121.

INTRODUCTION

The magnificent mountain ranges ringing the Puget Sound horizon have exerted a strong pull from the time of the earliest explorers. In the first years of the twentieth century, mountain travel was still difficult, but young men and women dreamed of reaching this remote and mysterious wilderness. The time was right for the birth of an outdoor club whose members could pool their energies to reach areas that individuals alone could not hope to visit.

The Mountaineers club, founded in 1906, resolved "to explore the mountains, forests and water courses of the Pacific Northwest, and to gather into permanent form the history and traditions of this region; to preserve, by protective legislation or otherwise, the natural beauty of the Northwest coast of America; to make frequent or periodical expeditions into these regions in fulfillment of the above purposes. Finally, and above all, to encourage and promote the spirit

A local walk on Spanaway Prairie near Tacoma (in 1923) included many prominent early leaders of The Mountaineers: Edmond S. Meany, Edward W. Allen, Leo Gallagher, Ralph Leber, Margaret "Hazzie" Hazard, Peter M. McGregor, Catherine Seabury, and Irving M. Clark. Local walks were a popular attraction from the start. Photo: Album, The Mountaineers Archives.

of good fellowship and comradery among the lovers of out-door life in the West."

These resolves remain as strong as ever—and this statement of purposes has even been expanded to reflect the club's growing role in the world at large. As The Mountaineers enters its tenth decade, this book tells the story of the first ninety years.

Headquartered in Seattle, today's Mountaineers has branches in five other Washington cities: Everett, Tacoma, Olympia, Bellingham, and Wenatchee. It owns clubhouses in Seattle and Tacoma, a forest preserve on the Kitsap Peninsula, and lodges at Snoqualmie Pass, Stevens Pass, the Mount Baker ski area, and near Stampede Pass. The club is also a major publisher of books on outdoor recreation and conservation.

The Mountaineers has had a profound impact on the Pacific Northwest and the larger outdoor community by providing a motivating philosophy and an organization for volunteers who work together for common goals. The club has built trails, mapped wilderness areas, and worked to preserve our natural treasure of forests, wild rivers, seacoasts, and wildlife habitats. Its support of wilderness values has helped secure legislation creating new public parks and protected areas.

Members of The Mountaineers introduced alpine skiing in the Northwest, encouraging downhill facilities and ski racing with gear and techniques fashioned for this part of the world. The club's mountain climbing course pioneered techniques of wilderness travel and safe ascents. Its classic climbing textbook, *Mountaineering: The Freedom of the Hills*, is used internationally.

The club didn't record all these accomplishments without occasional nudging from individual members who sometimes saw the value in such things as new climbing techniques or stronger environmental reforms before the organization itself did. And that's part of the strength of The Mountaineers, a big organization that at bottom is composed of individuals who find in the club a way to reach their own outdoor goals, whether it's expedition climbing or simply weekend hiking and boating.

More than fifteen thousand Mountaineers are now out and about, enjoying such pursuits as climbing, skiing, bicycling, and kayaking. And as they do, their club continues its effort to preserve the outdoor magnificence that surrounds us.

Chapter 1

GENESIS

The idea for The Mountaineers was conceived, appropriately enough, on a mountain. In 1906, two spirited young men came up with the notion of forming a Seattle mountaineering club while on a summer ascent of Mount Baker with a Portland, Oregon, outdoor group, the Mazamas. The men were W. Montelius Price, who would later start a successful electrical supply business in Seattle, and Asahel Curtis, a photographer known for his pictures of the Klondike gold rush. (His brother, Edward, won renown for photos of Pacific Northwest Indians.)

The two men had met the year before on Mount Rainier when Price, climbing with the San Francisco–based Sierra Club, bedded down for the night beside Curtis, who was with the Mazamas. The next spring they met again by chance in downtown Seattle, where Curtis urged Price to join him in a daring enterprise: an attempted first ascent of some major mountain in the Cascade Range before all of its tallest peaks had been climbed.

They decided on Mount Shuksan, a peak adjacent to Mount Baker near the Canadian border. They would join the Mazamas on that club's summer outing to Baker, then break off on their own to Shuksan. The outing lasted several weeks, so they had plenty of time to talk about forming a Seattle club. The conversation apparently was wide-ranging and included five or six other Seattle members of the Mazamas.

The first attempt on Shuksan by Curtis and Price had to be aborted when they ran into a sheer wall of rock. But they tried again and eventually made their way to the summit, Price lugging Curtis's 8-by-10 view camera and Curtis bearing the tripod and film plates. Seeing no sign that anyone had ever been there, they built a little cairn and sat on it for a summit photo. They are credited with the first ascent of Mount Shuksan, where the Curtis and Price Glaciers now honor their names.

The thought of forming a club lingered on, and that fall Curtis revived it in the downtown Seattle offices of physician Cora Smith Eaton. Her young office assistant, Mollie Leckenby, asked Curtis to take her along on one of his popular Sunday hikes, and Curtis commented, "Well, I guess we might as well start a small club of perhaps twenty folks. Dr. Landes of the university would be interested." Henry Landes, a University of Washington geology professor and state geologist, and his brother, Charles, had been among the Mount Baker climbers who had joined in debating the idea.

The biggest momentum for a club developed

Asahel Curtis and W. Montelius Price on the summit of Mount Shuksan during their first ascent in 1906. Curtis, a well-known photographer, rarely ventured forth without his 8-by-10 view camera, and this climb was no exception. He is renowned for his photos of Alaskan and Northwest mountain scenery. Price and Curtis first discussed the formation of a mountaineering club in Seattle during the Mazamas 1906 outing to Mount Baker. Photo: Asahel Curtis, Special Collections, University of Washington Libraries, neg. no. 7515.

after a local committee was formed to plan a reception for Dr. Frederick Cook, who was returning to Seattle from Alaska after his reported conquest of Mount McKinley. Cook was greeted in Seattle, the "gateway to Alaska," with great fanfare, including front-page newspaper accounts. Cook was taken at his word that he had made the first ascent of North America's highest mountain, and only later was his climbing route deemed unlikely and his story doubted.

The Cook reception seems to have gone off smoothly. But with that goal accomplished, the planning committee took on a life of its own and became the seed from which The Mountaineers grew. The reception planners— Eaton, Curtis, Dr. Weldon Young, and other local members of the Mazamas—met at the residence of Dr. E. F. Stevens and decided that a permanent committee was needed.

Its mission: to contact the Sierra Club and the Mazamas and determine what sort of club would be best for Seattle.

The historical basis for a mountaineering group already had been well established, with John Muir and others inspiring the Sierra Club's formation in 1892 and William Gladstone Steel working with friends to promote the Mazamas in 1894. The American Alpine Club, the Canadian Alpine Club, and the Alpine Club in London lent considerable respectability to such ventures. Many of the early members of the Mazamas had been in the Sierra Club, just as many of the early members of The Mountaineers were Mazamas. In fact, it was the original aim of The Mountaineers to become an auxiliary chapter of the Mazamas.

At a meeting of the new club held on January 18, 1907, in the Chamber of Commerce rooms in downtown Seattle, Henry Landes was elected president, Dr. J. P. Sweeney vice president, Dr. Cora Smith Eaton secretary, Dr. E. F. Stevens treasurer, and Mary Banks historian.

It didn't take long for word to get out. There was standing room only at the next meeting, on February 15, 1907, and 151 people enrolled as charter members. Besides the business of forming a new club, the highlight of the meeting was a lecture by an entomologist who had accompanied an expedition to Alaska. Clearly, mountain fever had taken hold in Seattle.

By that time, Curtis's "small club of perhaps twenty folks" had grown to 192 members. This created an organization of sizable proportions and great influence in young Seattle. Among the charter members were forty-two librarians and teachers, twenty-three businessmen, fourteen college professors, including eleven from the University of Washington, thirteen physicians and surgeons, three attorneys, two photographers, two bankers, and "Will" Steel, founder of the Mazamas and the man who would almost single-handedly promote creation of Crater Lake National Park in Oregon.

Entire families joined. Dr. John P. Sweeney and his wife signed up with their daughters Josephine and Mary. Henry Landes and his wife, Bertha (later to become Seattle's first and, so far, only woman mayor), joined along with Landes's brother, Charles. Asahel and Florence Curtis, plus Asahel's sister Eva, became members.

Slipping in just after the charter rolls closed

The Mountaineers "all in a line" on Glacier Peak during the 1910 summer outing. The original caption notes: "Puzzle: Find the women. They are all women." Photo: H. A. Fuller, Charles Albertson Photo Album, The Mountaineers Archives.

Always the academic, Edmond Meany writes in his journal during the 1911 outing to Mount Rainier, Mount Adams, and the Columbia River. Photo: A. H. Denman, Special Collections, University of Washington Libraries, neg. no. 18127.

was Edmond S. Meany, the engaging University of Washington history professor and lover of the outdoors who would become the guiding light of The Mountaineers for twenty-seven years.

The club continued to grow at quite an unexpected rate until by the end of 1907 it had 233 members, mostly Seattle residents but a few scattered in a great arc from Eastern Washington to Banff, Alberta; Minneapolis, Minnesota; Los Angeles, California; and Portland, Oregon. By November 15, 1907, the founders seem to have

realized what they had going. They altered the name of the club to reflect its wide appeal, calling it simply The Mountaineers and dropping the appended "Auxiliary to the Mazamas," which had been part of the original name.

It says a great deal about the quality of the early leaders that so many women felt secure in joining a club that had as its intention exploration of the wilderness. Out of the 151 charter members, 77 were women. From the beginning, women helped determine club policies, arranged trips and programs, kept records, and

Edmond Meany always led the Sunday morning worship service, and his son Ned was known for his wake-up bugle calls. This photo was taken at Spray Park on Mount Rainier during the 1924 outing. Photo: Mabel V. Nash, Special Collections, University of Washington Libraries, neg. no. 18154.

The "Six Peakers Graduation Dinner" during the 1931 summer outing to Mount Garibaldi in British Columbia saw club president Edmond S. Meany (center) honoring Mountaineers who had scaled Washington's six major glaciated peaks. Photo: A. H. Hudson, Harriet Walker Album, The Mountaineers Archives.

edited publications. Thanks in large part to The Mountaineers, both men and women made many first ascents in the Northwest mountains.

In keeping with the era, however, the organization was led by men, and they were the prime decision-makers. Also, it must be said that women usually were relegated to subordinate positions. But it was still a bit unusual in 1907 for men and women to associate as peers in a club setting.

It is further notable that in a period when there were so few female college graduates,

four of the women charter members were identified as "Dr.": surgeon L. Maud Parker, physicians Cora Smith Eaton and Sarah Kendall, and dentist Martha G. Covey. Physicians Myra L. Everly and Mary M. Mars joined later in 1907.

After a year as president, Henry Landes prevailed upon Meany, his fellow University of Washington professor, to take over. Meany was already well known to club members as a speaker at the monthly meetings. Meany knew Chinook, the native trading language, so the

Indian history he related at the meetings was authentic, augmented by items from his own collection of artifacts. He also presented accounts of pioneer history.

Just as Muir had been the Sierra Club's primary leader, and Steel the inspiration behind the Mazamas, so Meany would become the most powerful force in The Mountaineers. He retained the presidency until his death in 1935 from a stroke just before he was to teach a class at the university. Curtis and the others had organized the club and left their imprint on it, but Meany became the backbone of the organization.

Meany was born in East Saginaw, Michigan, in 1862 and came to Washington Territory with his family while he was still a teenager. During the summer of 1880, his father, who was working on a steamer on the Skagit River during a minor gold rush, fell overboard and drowned. This left Meany, not yet eighteen, as the principal support of his mother, sister, and baby brother.

To get by, Meany operated a tiny dairy, pasturing cows on grass that grew alongside Seattle's unpaved streets. He also got a job delivering newspapers, kept books for a grocer, and hired himself out as janitor at his church and at the only bank in town. The sheriff was so impressed by the young man's efforts that he stopped Meany on the street one day and told him that if he ever needed anything, he had only to ask.

Because of such support, Meany was able to enter the University of Washington, from which he graduated in 1885 at the top of his class. He became a reporter at the *Seattle Press*, then was promoted to city editor. During his tenure, the newspaper sponsored the Press Exploratory Expedition of 1889–90 into Washington's Olympic Range, and the explorers thought

enough of Meany to name a mountain after him. He would get the chance to climb his namesake peak on the first Mountaineers outing.

In 1891, Meany was elected to the state legislature and served for two sessions, during which he helped secure the University of Washington's current campus. The decision to move the school drew criticism because the original campus was conveniently located downtown, while the new one was way out at the end of a streetcar line. Meany may have argued for the new campus in part because of its spectacular views of the Cascades to the east, the Olympics to the west, and Mount Rainier to the south.

After his stint in politics, Meany became registrar at the university, then settled in as a history lecturer. He became head of the history department in 1897, a position he held for the rest of his life.

By 1907 Meany was ready for new challenges, and The Mountaineers fit in with his love of Indian lore, Northwest history, and the outdoors. In the club, he seems to have found the combination of pioneer individualism, romance, and academic application that suited him. "It was Meany who came to exemplify the ideals of The Mountaineers," the Washington Historical Quarterly reported in 1935 upon Meany's death.

Legendary stories about Meany abound.

According to a retrospective report in the 1956 *Mountaineer* annual, "On the 1920 Olympic outing the party was making a return trip down the Quinault River in canoes paddled by Indians. Always ready to exhibit his knowledge of their tongue, Professor Meany hailed a canoe carrying some Indians coming upstream and in his best Chinook asked how many of our canoes they had met. In the best of English came back the reply, 'Oh, about half a dozen.'

Edmond Meany (right), shown with his son Ned during the 1928 summer outing, was elected and reelected president of the club for a total of twenty-seven years, starting in 1908. Photo: A. H. Denman, Special Collections, University of Washington Libraries, neg. no. 18120.

"On another occasion while watching an Indian ceremonial, Professor Meany in his best jargon asked an Indian chap standing nearby the meaning of it all. Imagine his delight when back came the answer, 'Purely psychological.' "

Meany was devoted to the club and set very high standards of conduct, which many members felt it was their "privilege" to maintain. Meany "established standards of mountaineering ethics that have left a lasting imprint upon our organization—a priceless legacy. He gave so much dignity and prestige to the club that he made it outstanding in the nation," according to the Historical Quarterly.

Early members recalled Meany most clearly at campfires in mountain meadows. He was a natural-born storyteller, enriching members' appreciation of the locale by recounting its history and legends. He was also deeply religious and led Sunday services on summer outings.

Meany's engaging manner and kind attention to all club members, no matter how new, made him a beloved figure the club could rally behind during its formative years. The first thing newcomers often noted when coming into the club was the atmosphere of camaraderie mingled with deference to Meany.

Some people felt that twenty-seven years at the helm was too long, and that the club leadership had grown out of touch with the membership and with the changes in outdoor recreation brought about by the automobile. Upon Meany's death, the bylaws were revised so no president could serve for more than two years.

The Mountaineers in its early days was far ahead of many other organizations in social outlook, but it was not completely egalitarian. To join, each applicant needed endorsement by two current members. The applicants' names were then published in the *Mountaineer* bulletin and, if no one objected, the board of trustees accepted them as members.

The early organization was not truly open to diversification in other ways. If you didn't favor Protestant religious services, for example, you were out of luck. Meany led them, and his influence was pervasive. Or if you didn't like the military structure of the early walks and outings, you were unlikely to get along very well. And if you happened to be Native American or Chinese, it was unlikely you would even gain membership approval in the first place.

All of this was socially acceptable among most club members at the time, and it would be decades before they thought to change such notions. Members who chafed at such limitations kept quiet and accepted them as the price for a safe excursion into the mountains. During the 1960s and 1970s, as awareness of civil rights grew, the membership procedure was changed to welcome anyone fourteen years of age or older who agreed with the purposes of The Mountaineers and was willing to pay a small initiation fee and annual dues.

Chapter 2

INTO THE MOUNTAINS

The Mountaineers' legacy of outdoor adventures began with a local walk. Promptly at 9:30 A.M. on Sunday, February 17, 1907, forty-eight of the new club's members and guests began the trek to Fort Lawton, a military installation in what is now Seattle's Discovery Park. After greeting the captain of the fort, they proceeded on through the woods to the West Point lighthouse on Elliott Bay, made a campfire and ate lunch, then returned along the beach at low tide.

The group dressed for their walk as they might have for a Sunday picnic of that day, the women in long dresses and cartwheel hats, the men in dark suits, ties, and hats or caps. They were doing something unusual for the time, mixing men with women and young with old, and

∞

The first local walk, to the West Point light-house at Seattle's Fort Lawton, took place on February 17, 1907. The clothing may seem more appropriate for a church social, but maintaining decorum was of utmost importance at the time. Photo: The Mountaineer annual, 1907–08.

proper decorum was essential. Many of the later outings, even local walks, included overnight camps, which would be cause for scandal if not conducted with the utmost propriety.

Seattle was an ideal place for such walks, with so many pristine places close by, and they were soon scheduled every other weekend and attended by large groups of people. Participants often took a streetcar to the end of its line and struck out from there, or took a steamer across Lake Washington or Puget Sound to an isolated wagon track or trailhead.

"The numerous streetcar lines running out of Seattle, and its matchless waterways, including Lake [Washington] and [Puget] Sound, give opportunity for endless variety in the selection of route and objective point," Winona Bailey reported in the 1912 annual. "About once a month, a chartered steamer has carried one hundred to two hundred people across the Sound to some otherwise inaccessible spot, and waited to bring them back in the evening."

In the first two years, the club explored the entire shoreline of Lake Washington and the sparsely settled country south of the lake, followed many of the old trails around Bremerton and Port Orchard on the west side of Puget Sound, and visited the prairies between Tacoma and Olympia.

These local walks continue today in the form of the day hikes and climbs of current Mountaineers. But the walks were not the high point of the group's existence at the time. That distinction belonged to what the club officially termed its "summer outing." The summer outings were annual excursions, usually two or three weeks long, that fulfilled the club's purpose "to explore the mountains, forests and water courses of the Pacific Northwest." Activities on these outings were as varied as the members' interests, but almost always included a climb of

a major peak, naturalist walks, and photography, as well as shorter, easier climbs and walks in the vicinity of the base camp. Until a separate climbing course was set up in 1935, the summer outing also was where the club's mountaineering instruction took place.

Summer outings were massive undertakings, especially in the earlier years, considering the logistics of supplying food and equipment for scores of participants and the club's penchant for exploring where there were few access roads or trails. These annual outdoor extravaganzas were finally discontinued in 1980 due to competing activities and the realization that large groups of people camping together in the backcountry left environmental scars that were no longer acceptable.

THE FIRST SUMMER OUTING

Not long after the charter rolls closed, The Mountaineers set to work planning the first summer outing. The leaders were Asahel Curtis, Montelius Price, and Cora Smith Eaton. Their destination was the formidable Olympic Mountains.

The range on Washington's Olympic Peninsula was still terra incognita. The only exploration of note had been the Press Expedition of 1889–90 that was financed by Edmond Meany's employer at that time, the *Seattle Press*. Expedition members had returned with stories of amazing hardships. Seventeen years later, their accounts were still vivid in the minds of Mountaineers.

"Undaunted by the fact that every writer in referring to the Olympic region has always dwelt upon the impenetrability of the forests as the reason for its never having been explored, The Mountaineers soon after organization decided upon Mount Olympus as the goal of their first annual outing, with the idea of giving the members an opportunity for original research in a hitherto untouched field," club historian Mary Banks wrote in the 1907–08 annual.

However, a warning was given to the uninitiated: "There is no record of anyone having made the ascent of Mount Olympus. It should be distinctly understood that this excursion is to be a camping trip, and when the party has left Port Angeles there will be no hotels where meals or beds can be obtained."

Mount Olympus, at 7,965 feet, is the highest point in the Olympic Range. Its elevation isn't formidable, but its problems of access are. Surrounded by rain-forest valleys, Olympus receives enormous precipitation and has a vast system of glaciers despite its relatively low elevation. Climbers are often beaten back by snowstorms, which are as apt to occur in August as in January.

The proposed ascent attracted considerable press attention as the first attempt by any climbing club to scale the peak. Several well-known scientists asked to join the expedition to take advantage of the research opportunities. In fact, the outing added a second group, made up almost entirely of scientists.

Baggage was strictly limited. Each person was allowed just one cylindrical canvas bag not to exceed three feet in length and eighteen inches in diameter, weighing no more than thirty pounds. This requirement made packing rather tricky, given the reliance on heavy, bulky wool clothing. Musical instruments were exempt from the limits: the club wanted entertainment in camp.

And there were clothing requirements. Men were advised to have "one tramping suit of some good, stout material such as denim, khaki or corduroy. Women should have one durable waist (blouse) for tramping, and one to wear around camp. The skirt should be short, not much below the knee, and under it should be worn bloomers."

The idea of maintaining a dress code in the mountains may seem a bit silly today, but in the early days it was a fact of life. It would be years before women were permitted to wear pants on outings without causing a scandal. They were expected to wear their long skirts in camp and to change for the climb to shorter skirts worn over wool serge bloomers—uncomfortably hot garb for a summer climb.

Colored glasses were essential as protection from the sun. Women were advised to carry heavy veils to shield their faces from sunburn when on snow, while the men mostly used greasepaint to protect their skin.

The charge for that first outing was $40, or about two weeks' wages for the average working person. Transportation to Port Angeles by steamer was an additional $2.50 round trip. Each person also had to come up with three weeks away from work. But by 1907 wages were rising and vacation time was becoming an accepted part of the working world, so many salaried employees were able to consider the excursion.

Nowhere did Curtis or Price admit to any doubts that such an ambitious expedition could be carried out. Nevertheless, they must have been gladdened when a scouting team to Mount Olympus reported back: "The ascent did not appear to be very difficult and can undoubtedly be made by all who wish to do so."

To prepare for the undertaking, The Mountaineers organized a climb of Mount Si, which overlooks the town of North Bend, thirty-two miles east of Seattle. The 4,167-foot peak thus became the club's first official conquest.

The spirit of adventure was high on that Mount Si trip when on May 10, 1907, twenty-seven climbers left Seattle by train for the town of Snoqualmie. No passenger seating was available, so they rode in the baggage compartment. In Snoqualmie, the women retired to a hotel while the men slept on the floor of a vacant house. The area was rugged and lightly settled, so a guide was hired to lead them. Curtis and Price acted as "advance guards."

The ascent was tough enough that several members gave it up along the way, built fires, and waited for the rest to return.

"Our trail led ever upward, not wasting time in winding around the mountain flank, but growing steeper and steeper," Alida J. Bigelow wrote in the 1907–08 annual. "At times as the goal seemed almost impossible, the cheery words of comrades spurred us on, until at last we came to the end of the tatus [probably talus] slope and to the narrow chimney or rift through one of the pinnacles, and on up to the summit, reaching it at one ten."

The Mount Si climb tested the club's concept of organization along military lines. Each person was assigned to a company directed by a captain, usually aided by a lieutenant who brought up the rear and accounted for stragglers. Scouts were sent ahead to reconnoiter the route. There was even a bugler, who could be heard above the howl of the wind if retreat were required.

Such military order was considered essential from a logistics standpoint, and also because the climbing teams on the summer outings did not rope up. Curtis and other early leaders were aware of rope techniques in use in Europe at the time, but they avoided them for a number of reasons. The hemp ropes available then were unreliable and became stiff and unpliable in the cold; each team carried one for emergency purposes only or for use as a hand line. The leaders also realized that the use of ropes would have slowed a large party intolerably. And they found

it difficult enough to teach novices the techniques of self-arrest on snow, traversing ice, and climbing rock without adding rope handling. This approach appears to have been successful, and the club completed many demanding summer outings without fatalities.

The Mount Si expedition bolstered planning for the Olympus trip. But that first summer outing hit an obstacle when the organizers discovered that only elk trails existed into the heart of the Olympics, and these could not accommodate the pack train of horses that would carry supplies to the base camp. Ever resourceful, Curtis and others used their business savvy to persuade the Port Angeles Chamber of Commerce to cut a trail for them through many miles of forest, arguing that it would become an attraction for other parties and boost development of the area.

Then came another problem. Horse packers sought exorbitant prices for outfitting the expedition. Again the business acumen of Curtis and Price paid off. The club bought its own horses and resold them after the outing, even managing a profit.

And there was treachery. A guide hired to lead the trailblazers "had quietly made the ascent in advance of the club, and returning, had hastily published accounts of 'The Ascent of Olympus,' with no credit given the Mountaineers who had made the trip possible," according to L. A. Nelson, writing in the annual.

But this claim-jumper's luck didn't hold. A record of the "Parker party" ascent of July 17 was found on the Middle Peak of Mount Olympus, but the interlopers missed the true summit—the West Peak—of the three-pronged mountain.

Finally the day of reckoning came. On July 24, a group of sixty-five set out from Seattle for Port Angeles. They would be followed ten days later by another group of seventeen, mostly professors and scientists, led by club president Henry Landes. In Port Angeles, stagecoach rides were available for a dollar to those who did not want to walk the ten miles to McDonald, where the group planned to strike off into the wilderness. The newly cut trail led thirty miles along the Elwha River, deep into the unknown.

The climbers had been warned not to expect hotel food. In fact, meals composed entirely of hardtack, raisins, prunes, cheese, and chocolate had been recommended by an "authority" on these matters, an idea that was summarily rejected. The food on this and other outings turned out to be an event of its own. With one small camp oven covered by an awning, bread was baked every day and meals consisting of six courses or more were served to as many as sixty-five people.

A "steerage committee" was appointed to herd the roast-beef-to-be to base camp, but praises for any roast beef dinners are absent from the accounts. The trip was guaranteed to burn the fat off the steer and result in tough, stringy meat.

The group made some secondary ascents before reaching Olympus, including Mount Queets, Mount Seattle, Mount Barnes, and Mount Meany, with Edmond Meany climbing his namesake mountain for the first time. But it was the ascent of Olympus that had all the marks of a world-class climb, with a perilous first attempt and a near fatality.

Curtis describes an August 10 snowstorm that overtook the first summit attempt as "no ordinary snowstorm." It was a "thirty-mile gale" that dropped a foot of snow on the summit. "Three members of the party were exhausted, and it seemed folly to risk lives on the glacier in such a storm for the mere bauble of a mountain summit."

Winona Bailey and L. A. Nelson stood still long enough to have their picture taken during the 1930 outing to Mount Rainier. Bailey was a longtime board member, active in the "botany bunch," and one of the first to complete climbs of Washington's six major peaks. Nelson, after whom Little Big Chief Mountain is named, led the first ascent of Mount Olympus in 1907, was trip leader and climb leader on many outings over the next twenty-five years, and was the founding president of the Federation of Western Outdoor Clubs in 1933. Photo: Harriet Geithmann, Special Collections, University of Washington Libraries, neg. no. 18115.

The bugler sounded retreat, and the four companies fell into formation. "Through all of this, the discipline was perfect. Orders were obeyed as quickly as given; no one seemed to misunderstand and everyone appreciated the necessity for haste," Curtis wrote in the 1907–08 annual.

The strict military orientation probably accounted for the small number of accidents on the early outings. But there were some. On that first summit attempt led by Curtis, Winona Bailey lost her footing on the rain-soaked heather and fell over the rocks for a hundred feet, until she wedged under the snow at the base of a cliff. That her fall was not fatal seemed

miraculous to Dr. Stevens, who was acting as rear guard for Company D. He was called forward and "was working over the girl within five minutes after she fell."

Bailey was carried a half-mile down the slope on an improvised stretcher. "The task before the party was now tremendous, that of fitting up a hospital in a driving rain, without even a tent for shelter, and caring for a helpless girl ten miles from the main camp, with that camp sixty miles in the heart of the mountains.

"Here in this rude hospital, with the rain still falling, the main party was compelled to leave a small band to watch through the night and for days and nights to come, until it was possible to

❧

The first climbers to reach the highest point in the Olympic Mountains sit atop the west summit of Mount Olympus on August 13, 1907. The climb gained The Mountaineers instant respect and acclaim. Seated: Anna Hubert, C. E. Weaver, Henry Landes, A. W. Archer, and E. E. Richards. Standing: L. A. Nelson, W. Montelius Price, John B. Flett, F. M. Plumb, and Charles Landes. Photo: Theodore C. Frye, The Mountaineer annual, 1907– 08.

move her by stages to the main camp," Curtis continued.

Much was taken for granted in this account, since it was never explained how a shelter was rigged, what it was made of, or what comforts were provided for Bailey. These probably were details Curtis assumed everyone already knew. It would be two weeks before Bailey could be moved out of the mountains, but the experience didn't frighten her away. She remained active in The Mountaineers for many years and wrote articles on botany for club publications.

The second attempt on the summit of Olympus that summer was not nearly so eventful. It was accomplished with relative ease, on August 13, albeit without Curtis.

"Although hampered by storms, the party reached the summit without great difficulty and were rewarded by one of the grandest views to be had in the American mountains," noted L. A. Nelson, the climb leader.

The summit photo shows a group of slender, rugged-looking climbers, the one woman who accomplished the ascent as lean and fierce-looking as the men. The summit party was listed as Nelson, Anna Hubert, W. Montelius Price, E. E. Richards, A. W. Archer, and Professors Henry Landes, Charles Landes, T. C. Frye, F. M. Plumb, J. B. Flett, and C. E. Weaver.

Club historian Banks described the first summer trip as "probably the most wonderful outing ever taken by any mountain-climbing club." And so it must have seemed to those who participated in that historic expedition.

1908 MOUNT BAKER OUTING

By 1908, Mount Baker had been climbed numerous times, but the eastern side of the mountain was still believed to be inaccessible to large parties. To get to the intended base camp for that year's summer outing, an advance party built seven miles of trail. The outing committee spent ten days scouting the trail, selecting campsites, and negotiating for the thirty-two pack animals that would carry in supplies and dunnage.

The fifty-four members of the outing took the train from Seattle to the town of Baker (now Concrete) and camped the first night two miles from there. "It was a very dark night and we literally plunged into inky blackness, punctuated by improvised lanterns, called 'bugs,' constructed of tin cans and candles," Lulie Nettleton wrote in the 1907–08 annual.

The group followed the Baker River for fourteen miles, crossing a large number of streams, then followed a trail built by a resident miner—the fabled Joe Morovitz—to Boulder Creek, where it ended. From there, they took the new trail to timberline that the club had built between Boulder and Park Creeks.

Trees had to be felled to make a bridge over Boulder Creek. For Lulie Nettleton, the crossing was fearsome: "How the log topples. Your heart beats to suffocation and the water cries 'Come in! Come in! Come in!' A score of cameras leveled at one are disconcerting, too."

Dense huckleberry bushes made the intended main campsite unsuitable, so a mile-long path was cut to a desirable meadow. There, not one camp but two had to be established: one for the men and another for the women. Strict separation of the sexes in the tent areas was the rule, except for married couples.

The summit attempt on Mount Baker was made from a temporary camp at 5,000 feet elevation between Park and Boulder Glaciers. Behind the climbers, standing out against a brilliant sky, was 9,127-foot Mount Shuksan, which Curtis and Price had climbed two years before. Before them was 10,778-foot Mount Baker, renowned for its

A member of the "steerage committee" herds the camp's fresh meat across a stream during the 1908 trek to Mount Baker. Any praise of roast beef dinners is absent from members' accounts of the trip, probably because the animal lost all its fat on the strenuous trip to base camp. Photo: John A. Best, Jr., pamphlet, The Mountaineers Archives.

huge annual snowfall and the low elevations to which its glaciers descended.

"The Mountaineers' ascent of Mount Baker, made on July 29th with a party of thirty-nine, was remarkable only for the ease and safety from which this, the first large party, reached the summit," Asahel Curtis wrote in the 1907–08 annual. "Prior to this ascent, the climb of Baker had been considered very difficult, particularly with a large party, and no such party had succeeded in reaching the summit."

Curtis, who led the 1908 outing, had in a short time perfected the technique of military formation. One of his photos of the Baker climb shows a line of thirty-eight climbers, each not more than a single step behind the next, ascending

a steep snow slope. There was safety in numbers, with no one to rescue the climbers but themselves.

Their equipment was meager by modern standards. They used long alpenstocks instead of ice axes and had calks pounded into the soles of their leather boots for traction. Rescue gear was nonexistent, with the exception of a rope that someone carried along. Their survival depended on trust in the leader's routefinding abilities, and in one another.

The climbers carried only knapsacks, and some not even that. Hypothermia was not well understood at the time. Their clothing, as seen in Curtis's photos, was scarcely sufficient to save them from freezing if the weather changed or if one of them fell into a crevasse. They counted on other members of the party to lower clothing into the crevasse if anyone was unfortunate enough to plunge through a snow bridge.

For Curtis and the other experienced mountaineers, the climb must have been relatively easy, as the route lies off to the north side of Boulder Glacier on a rocky ridge and presents a straightforward line to the summit. The only technical difficulty was a cornice directly below the summit, where the snow had broken away, leaving a crevasse and a wall of snow twenty feet high to surmount. A snow bridge two feet wide was too thin to be safe.

This problem was resolved by chopping away at the snow cliff until it fell into the crevasse, thereby creating a bridge—a simple solution but one that only a party with large numbers could accomplish.

"As the sun reached its zenith, the last icy rampart had yielded and the great white peak is conquered," Nettleton wrote. "Mt. Rainier and Glacier Peak seemed only a stone's throw apart. A misty spot was pointed out as Puget Sound, and the Nooksack River looked like a tiny silver thread."

Curtis had led the 1906 party of 118 Portland Mazamas on the north side of Mount Baker and had failed to get more than 6 people to the summit. This time around he proved his organizing abilities by getting 39 people to the top, himself included. Mount Baker would never again be considered insurmountable by a sizable group.

Standing with the Mountaineers on the summit of Baker was Joe Morovitz, the "jolly hermit of Baker Lake," a gold prospector who had made lone ascents of the peaks in the area with such regularity that he never even bothered to build a cairn of rocks on the summits to mark his triumphs. His renown as a mountaineer began to spread after he helped the Mountaineers

pioneer their route between the Park and Boulder Glaciers. In fact, he'd already done that route himself, and when he stood with them on Baker's summit it was his seventh ascent.

Curtis and Price must have known that Morovitz had in all likelihood climbed Mount Shuksan when they claimed it for themselves in 1906, since it was virtually in his backyard. But Morovitz couldn't prove it, and at any rate didn't seem to care, since it failed to dampen his subsequent friendships with club members. Thereafter, the Morovitz ranch became a kind of headquarters for mountain climbers seeking guidance.

1909 MOUNT RAINIER OUTING

The summer outing to Mount Rainier was initially planned as a trip around the mountain. But that idea was abandoned after scouting trips found that trails on Rainier's north side hadn't been maintained or were elk paths leading nowhere. Of course, the Mountaineers could have gone to the south side, where access was assured, but it was the north side that hadn't been fully explored in 1909 and club members wanted the greatest challenge.

Mount Rainier National Park rangers advised building a trail through the Sluiskin Mountains, which guard the north end of the park, but this would have required a summer's work and cost fifteen hundred dollars. An alternative was a fifty-mile march up the White River Valley to Glacier Basin, which even the hardy Mountaineers didn't relish. The trail party determined to rebuild an old trail over the shifting moraine of the Carbon Glacier into the area known as Moraine Park. This feat was accomplished in a mere week's time.

The outing members left Seattle by train on July 17, 1909, got off at Fairfax near the northwest corner of the national park, and marched

Grant W. Humes was a guide during the first outing to the Olympics in 1907, an advance scout on Mount Baker in 1908 and Mount Rainier in 1909, a leader of the 1910 Glacier Peak outing, and an active Mountaineers member after that. He is shown on the 1913 outing to the Olympics. Photo: J. H. Weer, Special Collections, University of Washington Libraries, neg. no. 18129.

to the first camp eleven miles up the Carbon River trail. The next day the pack train arrived at Moraine Park.

"Here camp was established, quarters assigned to the men and women, the commissary housed in its own tents, and plans made for tryout trips. These served a double purpose, to see the surrounding country with the greatest possible dispatch and to drill members of the party and

try their mettle," Curtis wrote in the 1909 annual.

Curtis made a scouting trip with L. A. Nelson and Grant W. Humes up the Inter Glacier, a snout of ice and snow that descends off Steamboat Prow. He casually mentions in his write-up that a "broken shoulder" prevented him from going with Nelson and Humes to the summit. His collarbone had been fractured in a collision with a "lady" during a game of camp baseball.

The spot the men chose for their temporary camp is now known as Camp Curtis. It lies on a ridge of boulders and volcanic ash near Mount Ruth, between the Inter Glacier and what then was called the White Glacier, now the Emmons. While Nelson and Humes were blazing a route up the mountain, the other climbers arrived to bivouac on the open ridge, making themselves as comfortable as possible in the dirt and rock.

"Beds were made by laying a line of large rocks below to keep from rolling out and down the mountain. The looser earth was then dragged down to make a softer couch," Curtis wrote. He noted that the "greater part of the party had sleeping bags," indicating that blankets were still commonly used for covering up and trying to keep warm. Though sixty-two people stayed at this camp, seventeen others turned back once Nelson and Humes returned to tell how tough the climb was.

At 14,411 feet, Mount Rainier is the only mountain in Washington State tall enough to subject climbers to a true test of the rigors of high altitude. The account of the 1909 Mountaineers ascent differs little from that of climbers today. The main object by which elevation could be judged or distance measured was the nearby peak called Little Tahoma, an 11,138-foot pinnacle on Rainier's east ridge. As the climbers slowly toiled upward, they seemed to

Taken during the 1909 outing to Mount Rainier, this photo shows climbers moving along the inner slope of one of the summit craters. Photo: Charles Albertson Photo Album, The Mountaineers Archives.

gain so little on the elevation of this peak that the effect was disheartening.

At 12,500 feet, Curtis "passed along the line to see how everyone was taking it, and reached Dr. Van Horn at the head of company D. As he recognized me, he said: 'Curtis, this is no place for the father of eight children.' I could not help wondering how many more had reached the same conclusion."

In spite of his shoulder injury, Curtis managed to lead the climb up the huge volcanic mountain and to pack along his camera and take photos, including one of the party lunching in a crevasse at 13,000 feet.

"Once in the saddle between the summits, the ascent was easy, the entire party reaching the crater in eight hours and forty minutes from

temporary camp. Here, out of the wind, everyone sought a sheltered spot to warm themselves on the hot rocks and ashes."

The group descended to spend a second night at the temporary camp near Mount Ruth. "The following morning the clouds lay around the mountain in a vast sea that stretched on all sides to the horizon," Curtis wrote. "A few peaks broke through, but they were insignificant in comparison to the dominating bulk of ice that we were on. The impression was of being afloat on a great iceberg."

After the ascent of Mount Rainier, outing members made a side trip to Spray Park. "The park was so beautiful that it seemed unreal," noted Curtis, who could compare it with mountain vistas he had seen from California to

Alaska. "Nature had fashioned this playground much better than man could hope to, and had set it away here between two great glaciers at the base of a mighty mountain."

His conclusion: "It must always be the work of the club to assist in every way possible in the work of protecting the beautiful places of our state. A great part of this must be in educating those who, in greatly increasing numbers, go each year into the mountains."

1910 GLACIER PEAK OUTING

By 1910 and the fourth summer outing, the club had grown to four hundred members, of which seventy had the time and the means for an excursion to 10,541-foot Glacier Peak in the Cascades. Led again by Curtis, this too was a daring trip that evoked memories of the 1907 excursion to Mount Olympus. Only a handful of climbs of Glacier Peak had been recorded, none by a large party.

As was typical of climbs led by Curtis, the mountain was not approached from the "easy" west side, but from the east, on a route that involved many unknowns.

A surveyor's party led by Thomas Gerdine of the U.S. Geological Survey had been the first up the mountain, in 1897. His route was followed the same year by I. C. Russel. In 1906, a route was pioneered up the east side by Claude Rusk and A. L. Cool. The fourth ascent was made by a Mountaineers scouting party led by L. A. Nelson, with the object of cruising out the

The Mountaineers "climbed in pockets and on ledges" up and over the ice cliffs of Mount Rainier's Carbon Glacier on July 26, 1909.
Photo: Charles Albertson, Charles Albertson Photo Album, The Mountaineers Archives.

A group on top of 10,541-foot Glacier Peak on August 5, 1910, gathers around the summit record box. They're wearing blue glasses to prevent snow blindness and greasepaint to prevent sunburn. A. H. Albertson (in the foreground), a prominent architect, was greatly influenced by his mountain experiences, writing in the 1929 Mountaineer: "On the Glacier Peak outing of 1910, I was struck by certain rock masses which suggested architectural form." Seattle's Northern Life Tower, designed by his firm in 1929, strongly reflects that influence. Photo: Charles Albertson, Charles Albertson Photo Album, The Mountaineers Archives.

best route for the club's group climb. Following them were a Dr. Hall and a Dr. Dehn of the University of Washington. The sixth ascent was made by Mountaineers on the 1910 outing, "fifty-seven in line."

Permanent camp was established at Buck Creek Pass, a high alpine park of extraordinary beauty. The pass was approached by a series of four temporary camps and a walk of forty-four miles after leaving the train at Nason Creek, about twenty miles west of Leavenworth on the east side of the Cascades.

The route to the peak extended from Buck Creek Pass southwest to the Suiattle River, crossing that and the Chocolate River, then leading back up to timberline. The ascent route crossed the Cool Glacier to an arête between the Chocolate and Cool Glaciers. It was another straightforward summit climb, accomplished without incident, well planned and scouted.

Life in the camp for the three weeks the Mountaineers stayed was as invigorating as the climb. Lulie Nettleton wrote in the 1910 annual:

"One of the most delightful features of the club outings are the campfires. Here we used to gather each evening like fire worshipers of old, with President Meany to lead in the ceremonial. He would tell weird tales of the Indians, or stories of the early explorers who made history in our great Westland, or perhaps he would read verses from his own pen, inspired by the scenery or by some dainty mountain flower. . . .

"Certain evenings were devoted to real frolics. Particularly memorable was the night when Miss Gotlotsofgreenbacks was joined in mock matrimony to my Lord Montague de Montmorency by the Rev. Rockandrye. The ring bearer, flower girls, bridesmaid, best man, bride's mother and bride and bridegroom were all of the masculine gender, most gloriously arrayed; and as the bride came in, to the strains of Lohengrin's 'Wedding March,' with eyelashes dropped demurely upon bearded cheek, the whole company were very much affected."

The camp even had its own violinist, Margaret Coenen, who awakened them with "strains of music so exquisite as to seem part of a lovely dream."

On the summit of 14,411-foot Mount Rainier in 1912, with the club banner unfurled.
Photo: P. M. McGregor, Special Collections, University of Washington Libraries, neg. no. 18113.

Left: During the 1911 outing, the glaciers of the Goat Rocks were crossed in company formation. On the steeper slopes "captains" and "staff officers" were stationed below to rescue any climber who slipped and started to slide down the slope. The club never had a fatality while using these techniques.
Photo: R. J. Hageman, Special Collections, University of Washington Libraries, neg. no. 18126.

Above: On the summit of Mount Olympus during the 1913 outing: Winona Bailey, H. May Baptie, Grace Howard, Lulie Nettleton, P. M. McGregor, and L. A. Nelson. All had been on the first 1907 summer outing to the Olympics. Photo: P. M. McGregor, Special Collections, University of Washington Libraries, neg. no. 18159.

Left: A climbing party ascends Mount Seattle during the 1913 outing to the Olympics. Note the use of alpenstocks; ice axes were not yet in wide use. Photo: P. M. McGregor, Special Collections, University of Washington Libraries, neg. no. 15263.

Chapter 3

REVOLUTION

The annual summer outing was the major focus of the club's climbing activities and the occasion of most of its climbing instruction for almost thirty years. Although climbing wasn't specifically stated as a club purpose, it was taken for granted as a fundamental aim. The Mountaineers early on acknowledged mountaineering achievement, and by the 1920s was publicly taking note of members who had attained six prominent summits in Washington—Mounts Rainier, Adams, Baker, St. Helens, and Olympus, and Glacier Peak. In 1921, seventeen club members were designated as "graduate members" for having climbed the six majors.

However, for many charter members, the key word in the purpose statement was "explore," and Washington State's mountains weren't fully explored even as late as the 1930s. Numerous trails led out of the lowland valleys of the Olympics and the Cascades, but climbers' paths to higher base camps were usually nonexistent, and once off the trail the going was tough as climbers had to battle devil's club, vine maple, slide alder, and fallen trees.

The evolution of club climbing techniques began not long after the group's founding, accelerated with the opening of Snoqualmie Lodge in 1914, and has continued to the present day. The lodge quickly became a social and climbing center in addition to a focal point for winter sports. Nearby peaks were designated and members strove to qualify for pins that recognized ascents of the "First Ten" and "Second Ten" peaks.

Climbers in the young organization quickly began to look for opportunities beyond those of the annual summer outing. This interest first coincided, then conflicted, with policies relating to Snoqualmie Lodge, the club's first piece of real estate.

SNOQUALMIE LODGE AT LODGE LAKE

The idea of a lodge in the mountains was first discussed around a campfire in the Elwha Basin during the 1913 summer outing to Mount Olympus. The proposal was so attractive it was put to a vote on the spot, and the motion carried with enthusiasm.

Back in Seattle, a study group began looking into what other mountain clubs in the United States and Europe had done by way of lodges. The only thing that came even close to what The Mountaineers envisioned was the Sierra Club's Muir Lodge in Big Santa Anita Canyon near Los Angeles. But that lodge was built for a

The "graduating class of August 1921," Karen Olsen, Laurie Frazeur, O. J. Smith, Linda Coleman, and Crissie Cameron, stands on the summit of Glacier Peak, having completed their climbs of Washington's six major glaciated peaks. At the time, climbing was taught almost exclusively during the summer outings. Photo: O. J. Smith, Special Collections, University of Washington Libraries, neg. no. 18119.

The original Snoqualmie Lodge at Lodge Lake was virtually a second home for many Mountaineers. Sitting before the lodge in 1930: Rudy Amsler, Priscilla Story, Jim Martin, Norval Grigg, Margaret Bearse, and Gloria Huntington. Photo: Larry Byington, The Mountaineer annual, 1956.

different climate, and the design was far from adequate for Cascade Mountains snow loads.

This led Irving Clark, secretary of the lodge committee, to report in the 1913 annual "that not a great deal of the data bears on the Mountaineer lodge problem, and that we will, therefore, have to solve it alone."

The Mountaineers did solve the problem alone, and in characteristic fashion, through volunteer effort on a grand scale. Here is where The Mountaineers' tradition of volunteerism got its start, and much of the club's success over the years is attributed to volunteer involvement arising from the pioneer ethic of working together.

It didn't take much study to conclude that the lodge would have to be situated in the Cascades, since the Olympics were far less accessible, especially in winter. And in the Cascades, the Snoqualmie Pass area was the easiest to reach because of rail access.

The railroads were still competing for fares at the time and would drop passengers off or stop and pick people up at remote whistle-stops. A drawback to this informal arrangement was that users of the eventual lodge sometimes had to stand out in bad weather for hours, waiting for a train that was late.

The site selected for the lodge was about halfway between the Chicago Milwaukee

Railroad station at Rockdale (at the western end of Snoqualmie Tunnel, which was then under construction) and Snoqualmie Pass. The land, rented from the U.S. Forest Service, was at an elevation of 3,200 feet near a small lake, named Lodge Lake by The Mountaineers, a name later accepted as official by the U.S. Geological Survey. Denny and Granite Mountains dominated the view across the valley.

The original Snoqualmie Lodge was built on a knoll about a quarter-mile southwest of the lake. The structure was made almost entirely of materials found on the site, including logs that were peeled, cedar that was turned into roof shakes, and stones for a huge fireplace. The main room measured 30-by-34 feet, and there was an adjacent kitchen and women's dorm on the first floor. The men's dorm was in the attic over the main room. There was no electricity or plumbing, but that was not considered a hardship.

The lodge was designed by Carl Gould, one of the nation's finest architects and a Mountaineers member. It was a work of art in which members took enormous pride. One volunteer, Professor S. L. Boothroyd, was so enthusiastic

Mountaineers skating on Lodge Lake on November 3, 1935: Gilbert Erickson, Edna Turner, unknown, Dorthea Blair, Evelyn McAlpine, and Forrest Farr. Farr was one of the best climbers of his time, with first ascents of Big Four, Chimney Rocks, Dome, and Three Fingers. Photo: Art Winder collection, The Mountaineers Archives.

The original Snoqualmie Lodge was reached by a long hike up a slope after being left off by the train, at a time when trains would still stop to pick up passengers waiting alongside the tracks. But it could be a long, cold wait as the trains didn't always run on time. Here a group from the lodge waits at Rockdale Station, located at the west portal of the Milwaukee Railroad tunnel. Photo: Fairman B. Lee, Special Collections, University of Washington Libraries, neg. no. 18137.

he brought his entire family to the site during the summer of 1914 so they could devote themselves exclusively to working on the building.

"Other enthusiastic members worked in their spare time, and by the last of August the building was closed up and ready for use without hiring help, with the exception of one week when two carpenters were hired to put in doors and windows and to make window seats," Sidney Bryant reported in the 1914 annual.

Until the early 1920s, Snoqualmie Lodge was primarily a climbers' lodge, used as a starting point for ascents of the surrounding peaks, including Snoqualmie, Guye, Kendall, the Tooth, Chair, Red, Denny, and Silver. It was through the lodge that new members first learned to climb and earned their ten-peaks pins, indicating they had climbed one or two groups of ten of the nearby mountains. The lodge also was a social center.

"Climb or hike all day and dance all night," David Lee noted in a retrospective report in the 1977 annual. "The wind-up Victrola horn got plenty of use."

The Snoqualmie Pass area was still fairly remote before the highway was opened all winter for the first time in 1931, and getting to the lodge took time. The journey involved a train excursion from Union Station in Seattle to Rockdale, which was more than a mile from

On a cross-country ski trip to Mount Margaret near Snoqualmie Pass in the 1930s: Edna Walsh (in foreground), Carl Lindgren, Arthur Wilson, Don Blair, Clarke Marble, Walter Hoffman, Walter Nicholson, and Gertrude and Paul Shorrock. Photo: Art Winder collection, The Mountaineers Archives.

the lodge. Members hiked the rest of the way.

"Many have asked why, in these early days, was the Lodge built in a location that today would seem remote and inaccessible. A steep 1¼-mile climb from the old Denny Creek Ranger Station during the summer months or a 1⅔-mile struggle over snow-covered trails from Rockdale station during the winter time was required to reach our 'mountain home,' " Larry Byington wrote in the 1956 annual.

"For those of us who knew and loved the old Lodge, no explanation is required. For others who have come later, it may be difficult to explain. Perhaps it will suffice to say that the far-sighted

planners of the Lodge believed that a club dedicated to the love and preservation of the out-of-doors should maintain a lodge far removed from the artificiality of busy highways, railroads and crowded resorts."

The train trip was a lark compared with car excursions in the days before highways over the pass were paved. Then the drive was a four-hour ordeal. To reach Snoqualmie Pass from Seattle it was necessary first to drive through the Seattle suburbs of Lake City, Lake Forest Park, Juanita, Kirkland, and Redmond before negotiating narrow country roads to Snoqualmie Falls and North Bend. From there the road wound slowly upward, with the destination either a parking lot across from Lodge Creek just below Lodge Lake, or the pass itself.

And that was in the summer. A winter trip meant tire chains and the ever-present danger of sliding into a ditch.

Nevertheless, for nearly thirty years the lodge was among the most important institutions of the club. It was not only a base for climbing but became a development center for skiing.

On the negative side, the lodge's cost of operation became a sore point. And climbers came to dislike the rules that said they had to sign in at the lodge before going on *any* climbs, which effectively restricted climbing to the Snoqualmie Pass area. The climbers had to drive up to the little lot or park along the highway and hike the steep switchbacks to the lodge, all for the privilege of signing in and out and paying a surcharge for doing so, even if they didn't use the lodge. Despite these fees, the

T. R. Conway, Elizabeth Wright, Lulie Nettleton, Helen MacKinnon, Norm Engle, Edith Knudson, and L. A. Nelson at Snoqualmie Lodge, April 20, 1920, a time when winter sports were just beginning to catch on. Photo: Rodney L. Glisan, Special Collections, University of Washington Libraries, neg. no. 18142.

Gordon Pole   F.B.L.   Joe Hazard (Mgr)   Alma Wagen   Jake Shidell (summit)   Hans Führer (summit)

The Guide Dept — Paradise Inn — 1919

In 1919, the guide service on Mount Rainier consisted of Gordon Pole, Fairman B. Lee, Joseph Hazard,
Alma Wagen, Jake Shidell,* and Hans Führer.* Asahel Curtis inaugurated the guide service in 1917,
and The Mountaineers furnished the first four guide managers. Lee led the first ascent of Mount Anderson
in the Olympics in 1930 and chaired the Cascade Trail Committee after its founding in the early 1930s.
Hazard was a driving force in the designation of the Pacific Crest Trail and was a frequent visitor to
Kitsap and Snoqualmie Lodges. Photo: Frank Jacobs, Special Collections,
University of Washington Libraries, neg. no. 18114.

lodge nearly always required an annual appropriation from the general fund, which further rankled diehard climbers.

Renowned Northwest climber Herman Ulrichs, a club member from 1927 to 1933, dropped out partly over dissatisfaction with lodge rules.

"One reason I left The Mountaineers," he told Karyl Winn in a 1973 interview, "was that they had this lodge at Snoqualmie, and it was the patriotic thing among all the Mountaineers to patronize the lodge. So they organized a series of 10 peaks that everyone was supposed to climb, and when they climbed them, they organized a second 10 peaks series, and when you got through that you were supposed to do them all over again. And I looked at the various maps of the Cascades, and there seemed to me many

Lines of climbers make their way up the slopes of Mount Olympus during the 1913 outing. Early Mountaineers could rely only on themselves for rescue and there was safety in numbers. Photo: Rodney L. Glisan, Special Collections, University of Washington Libraries, neg. no. 18128.

more interesting places than Snoqualmie Pass. But The Mountaineers were devoted to keeping this lodge going financially, and they didn't want to climb anywhere else."

OUTLAW CLIMBING

"In increasing numbers our members have scrambled up new creek beds, over slippery heather slopes, through hanging rock chimneys to new aeries," wrote Joseph T. Hazard in the 1917 annual. "Many are frankly interested in first ascents, in speed records, in endurance tests."

What Hazard was revealing, whether he knew it or not, was the dawn of the era of small-party climbing in The Mountaineers. "No longer are we at the mercy of the accident of a three-week's vacation. We have at our command an amazing variety of activities that may be contracted into the few swift hours from Saturday to Monday morning," he continued.

Hazard must have sensed that he was treading

on thin ice politically, because he quickly added, "The weekend trip will never be a rival of the Summer Outing. It is complementary."

During the 1920s, a restless body of young people who sought year-round activities was drawn to The Mountaineers, and many of these independent members banded together to climb unsanctioned by the club. This trend was at first called "outlaw climbing" by established members. Moreover, these climbers resisted being forced to pay the user fee charged for the maintenance of Snoqualmie Lodge, and the rules requiring registration before climbs.

In the 1920s and early 1930s, the club leadership reflected the interests of an aging, tradition-bound generation. The much-revered Edmond Meany remained as president long past the time when it would have been wise to turn leadership over to more forward-looking members. He and his fellow officers were fundamentalists, devoted to a literal interpretation of the club's purpose statement. And nowhere did it mention

Before participants in summer outings could embark on a major climb, they were given training on snow and rock during tryout trips such as this one on Glacier Peak in 1921. The members are divided up into six "companies," distinguished only by the slight space between each group. Photo: Frank J. Jones, The Mountaineer annual, 1921.

climbing as a distinct purpose.

The summer outing still was the main climbing event of The Mountaineers' year, but that was changing. The peaks around Snoqualmie Lodge, with their steep rock faces and large seasonal snowfields, required a variety of climbing techniques that, once learned, inevitably led climbers deeper into the Cascades and on to greater technical difficulties. As climbers kept seeking new heights, the club had no real control over how these climbs were organized and led. It wouldn't be until 1930 that the club's first climbing committee was established in an attempt to direct these activities.

These early young climbers were expected to adhere to a climbing gospel that had been revealed in 1906. Then, skilled leaders and skilled climbers were few, and the European method of roping each novice to an experienced guide was not practical because there were not enough guides to go around. Besides, few knew anything about rope techniques anyway. The methods developed by Asahel Curtis, L. A. Nelson, and others combined roped-in scouting by an exploring party with securely anchored fixed ropes at all danger points for the main climbing party, which was necessarily large since almost all of the real climbing was concentrated within the two to three weeks of the summer outing.

"Climbing in large groups, as we do in our Western mountains, has developed certain methods not used in other regions where the guides take only small parties," Nelson noted in the 1923 annual. "The guides in Europe and the Canadian Rockies rope their people, while we do not. Our method is to stretch ropes anchored to alpenstocks or ice axes. These act as a handrail in ticklish places. The effect is psychological in that the climber gains confidence he may lack without the rope."

Hazard noted in a 1937 annual retrospective that these techniques were revolutionary for their time. "These new methods were successful and were the marvel of the day to those clubs that had never faced the responsibility of large groups of unskilled enthusiasts, with few to lead them."

The early techniques worked splendidly for large groups of novices. In 1919, the club could boast that it had "never yet lost a man." Or a

On top of The Tooth just above Snoqualmie Pass in 1927: William J. Maxwell, unknown, Paul Shorrock,
and Larry Byington. Note the manila rope. Stretchable Perlon ropes were still a long way off.
Photo: W. J. Maxwell, Special Collections, University of Washington Libraries, neg. no. 18147.

woman, for that matter. The first recorded death of a club member while climbing—that of Carrie Lewis, who slipped and fell near Monte Cristo in 1921—did not occur during a club event.

Leaders such as Nelson were also partly correct in avoiding ropes since they had heard stories of a single climber's slip pulling an entire rope team to their deaths.

But for Hazard and others, the summer outing wasn't enough. The mountains didn't beckon just three weeks out of the year, but year-round. Although he noted in 1917 that climbing techniques were becoming more refined, there was no organized teaching of techniques, except for the preparatory sessions at the summer outings. The only alternative was to ferret out an experienced climber who would tutor you. But while expert climbers were few, those willing to teach were even fewer.

During the 1920s, climbing techniques were often looked upon as secrets that novices learned only at their peril. This was in part because the older climbers had a vast mountain playground full of virgin peaks at their disposal and didn't want to be bothered with inexperienced climbers, and partly because they genuinely feared for the safety of the novices.

At the same time, accounts of first ascents were being read with avid interest by club members. One such description was of the first ascent of Mount Constance in the Olympics on June 26, 1922, by A. E. Smith and Robert Schellin, as recorded in the 1922 annual:

"Mr. (Thomas J.) Acheson's ten-power binoculars revealed a succession of almost perpendicular rock walls, which promised some real climbing for any party who should ever reach the top.

"As we had decided our route the previous night, we lost no time on the 1,500-foot wall that rose in front of us. This wall was cracked in a manner that made climbing easy.

"About 500 feet higher we reached the top of the ridge at a point where a vein of red and very rotten rock crossed. Our course lay along the ridge and, as there was no other choice, we had to cross it. One side broke sheer away with no possible footing, the other was a steep slope of fifty or sixty feet ending in a cliff. A rope would have been a great help here, but we had not taken one on this trip. I believe it took us half an hour to cross that fifty-foot vein.

"As the climb up had really been hard, we decided to go down the north or opposite side of the ridge. We regretted this afterwards, but as we were both alive at the bottom it was probably well we went that way. Once down neither of us was extremely eager for another climb of the same mountain."

Such accounts pointed up the excitement of a first ascent, but they also showed the risk involved. Climbing without a rope *was* a bit foolhardy, even if a rope wasn't much use to climbers who had no idea how to use it other than to string it out as a hand line.

The same went for other climbing gear. Pitons were generally in use in Europe by the 1920s, but the Mountaineers, being climbing purists who felt aids of any kind should be avoided, regarded them as heresy. Standing around a campfire during the 1925 summer outing to Mount Stuart, the modernist Joe Hazard spoke of his attempt at the "sheer and inaccessible" summit of Chimney Rock and then had the effrontery to suggest use of pitons: "I will climb it if someone will go ahead and plant iron spikes in the rocks." He was greeted with howls of derision.

"However popular these contrivances may be in Switzerland and other well-known mountain regions, one of the happiest features of this

≪∞≫

Wolf Bauer gives a rappel demonstration to other club members in 1936 on Little Si near North Bend. Standing shirtless is William A. "Bill" Degenhardt. The dulfersitz rappel was used, even for sheer rock faces, as harnesses were unknown. Degenhardt, who helped establish the climbing course in the late 1930s, explored the southern Picket Range and made the first ascent of Mount Terror in 1933 with Herb Strandberg and Jim Martin. He was a longtime club leader, and among his first ascents was Peak 8200 in the Pickets, now named Mount Degenhardt in his memory. Bauer, in addition to helping start the climbing course and making a number of impressive first ascents, was a champion skier and in 1948 founded both the Seattle Mountain Rescue Council and the first kayak club in the Northwest. Photo: Wolf Bauer, The Mountaineer annual, 1968.

entire area of mountain architecture is the fact that there are as yet no iron spikes, no modern aids to mountaineering," William Seymour boasted in the 1925 annual.

One early climber, Norval Grigg, confessed to Malcolm Bates in the book *Cascade Voices*

that in the 1920s even those climbers who knew enough to bring a rope didn't know what a rappel was, so couldn't use the rope to descend easily and safely. "We just looped the rope over a knob in the rock or something. We just had two strands of rope and we'd slide down. You had to have sure hands and feet," Grigg said.

By 1930, climbing was moving beyond the limits of technique that the club was providing. Climbing could no longer be relegated to summer outings, and peak baggers were out to make their way up some of the most difficult ascents in the Cascades and Olympics.

Chimney Rock in the Dutch Miller Gap area, which had foiled Hazard in 1925, was first climbed in 1930 by Art Winder, Laurence Byington, and Forrest Farr. They made the ascent without ropes or crampons, using steps hacked into the ice. Farr and Winder did their rock climbing in rubber-soled shoes. Byington, who had only nailed boots, took them off and climbed in his stocking feet. Finally, to get more friction, he finished the climb in bare feet.

In the 1932 annual, Herbert Strandberg recounts a scouting trip to the Picket Range in an article titled "Ten Days on Mount Terror," and the following year James Martin, William Degenhardt, and Strandberg made the first ascent. A second ascent of Terror was not made for another twenty-eight years.

The action was heating up and the club knew it. Leaders could no longer sit back and lecture climbers on the joys of the summer outing while members were heading off on their own to some of the most difficult peaks in the Cascades equipped with little more than perseverance and luck.

The club wasn't serving the needs of ambitious young climbers such as Lloyd Anderson, who was among those balking at the requirement to check in at Snoqualmie Lodge. The country

was in the throes of the Depression, spending money was scarce, and climbers resented having to use part of their precious free time from work (usually half a day on Saturday and all day Sunday) to sign in at the lodge. Committed climbers began squeezing in two or three peaks on a single weekend. Anderson, in just his first two years of climbing, achieved all six of the state's major peaks and all twenty of the Snoqualmie peaks for which pins were awarded.

In 1934—the year before Meany's death—some of these members came together to organize what they called the climbers group. They essentially contended that old-time members were holding the younger ones down with a climbing schedule restricted mainly to the peaks surrounding Snoqualmie Lodge and the six majors and by not sharing their knowledge of climbing techniques. They started a revolution that would change the focus of the club and orient it toward climbing.

THE CLIMBING COURSE

This revolution was not a minor rumble. The first meeting of the new climbers group, on September 25, 1934, drew thirty-five members— 7 percent of the club's total membership—and the vote to organize was unanimous. Though the group was not officially recognized by the club, it proceeded as if it were.

At the group's first regular meeting two weeks later, John E. "Jack" Hossack was elected leader, William Degenhardt rear guard, and Jane Wing registrar. A call was issued stating that "any Mountaineer desiring to belong to this promising organization" could join for the nominal fee of twenty-five cents a year, "provided the member is actively interested in mountaineering."

The following year, the climbers group, still

The first ascent of Eldorado Peak in the North Cascades was achieved on August 27, 1933, by (bottom to top) Don Blair, Art Wilson, and Arthur Winder, along with Norval Grigg, who was taking the picture. Winder was a member of the club for sixty years. In addition to almost single-handedly conducting The Mountaineers conservation program for many years and assuming numerous leadership positions within the club, he was known as a swift, strong climber, with first ascents of Chimney Rock in 1930, Big Four Mountain and Three Fingers in 1931, Gothic and Eldorado Peaks in 1933, and Storm King in 1935. Photo: Art Winder collection, The Mountaineers Archives.

George MacGowan offers a demonstration of climbing technique during the 1939 summer outing to the Grand Tetons in Wyoming. He and Jack Hossack made the first ascent of the Grand by way of the northeast couloir on that trip. Both were instrumental in starting the climbing course. MacGowan also made first ascents of Mount Goode in 1936, Mount Challenger in 1938, and Spire Point in 1939.
Photo: Mary Grier, Special Collections, University of Washington Libraries, neg. no. 18141.

Agnes Dickert and Othello Phillip Dickert on a spring hike in the early 1930s. Both were enthusiastic climbers. Agnes reached sixteen summits in one summer, made the first ascent of Blue Mountain (since renamed Gunsight Peak) with Lloyd Anderson and Lyman Boyer, and was the first woman to climb Big Four Mountain. Othello, who took numerous photos of the Players and other Mountaineers activities through the 1980s, made first ascents of Mount Challenger and Mount Goode, both in 1936, and Spire Point in 1938. Photo: O. P. Dickert collection.

without official sanction, began the first climbing course, with monthly meetings and lectures focused on the problems climbers should be prepared to face. Wolf Bauer, a young University of Washington engineering student, gave the lectures and demonstrations and led field trips to Lundin Peak near Snoqualmie Pass and to Mount Si. Attendance at these sessions was compulsory for the students, who had to pass a stiff exam given by Bauer.

In a 1980 interview for the *Mountaineer* annual, Bauer noted the dissatisfaction of climbers of his generation with the older mountaineers.

"People like Forrie [Forrest] Farr, Art Winder, Norval Grigg had learned climbing the hard way, their own way. They had never seen a piton before. They were doing shoulder belays. They were older and were sort of a clique. They kept to themselves. When I got in, they would never teach me anything. I was just an upstart, a kid. They believed you had to learn it yourself. It was because of that I felt somebody should be teaching mountaineering techniques and not holding it to themselves."

Bauer was asked to teach the course along the lines of a climbing class he already was

Mountaineers on the summit of McClellan's Butte in the early 1930s. Standing: Harry Jensen, unknown, unknown, unknown, O. Phillip Dickert, Lloyd Anderson, Mary Anderson, T. Davis Castor, and Jack Hossack. Seated: unknown, Bill Miller, unknown. All those named in the back row were instrumental in setting up the climbing course in 1936 and assumed club leadership several years later. Hossack made first ascents of Ptarmigan Ridge on Mount Rainier in 1934, Mount Goode in 1936, Mount Challenger in 1938, and the northeast couloir of the Grand Teton (Wyoming) in 1939. He was also involved in the formation of the nation's first Mountain Rescue Council in the 1940s. Photo: O. P. Dickert.

conducting for the Explorer Scouts. Bauer had come to Seattle as a boy from Germany and had written to friends there asking for up-to-date information on mountaineering. When the German materials arrived, he says, "I really took fire. I studied those books and then went out and practiced all by myself, until I had some of the new techniques down pat." Many of the techniques Bauer introduced were generally unknown in the United States.

He made his first rappel off the girders of a city bridge, and that same evening lowered himself three stories down the central shaft of the Rialto Building, which housed The Mountaineers clubrooms, while his climbing students lined the railings to watch his descent to the marble floor below. It would be many years before harnesses came into use, and Bauer used the dulfersitz rappel in which the rope is wrapped around the body.

Bauer admitted he was "scared as hell going down that thing," then adds with a note of dark humor, "The marble slab was all laid out for me at the bottom in case anything happened." But there were no slips, and the students were much impressed.

This initial course was so successful that for the following year, the climbers group planned sessions for both beginners and advanced students.

By this time, it was evident to anyone who had been reading the *Mountaineer* annuals that independent climbing throughout the Cascades and Olympics had begun to overshadow the mass climbs of the summer outing. The 1933 annual, a slender forty-page Depression-era volume, managed to get in "The Ascent of Eldorado Peak," "An Attempt at Ptarmigan Ridge on Mt. Rainier," and "The Climbing Guide" on the climbing group's first effort at drawing up a plan. Edmond Meany's description of the club's fifth outing into the Olympics, although pleasant enough, couldn't compete with the climbing accounts for drama.

In spite of this, the old guard appears to have remained adamant in its fight to retain control of climbing, especially the requirement that climbers pay a fee at Snoqualmie Lodge, presumably even if the climb was as distant as Eldorado Peak in the North Cascades. They felt, with some justification, that without these climbing fees, the club would become insolvent.

The younger climbers were left with two options: form their own club or get involved in club politics. They chose the latter and in 1937 put up four candidates for the board: George MacGowan, Lloyd Anderson, Harry Jensen, and Agnes Dickert. All four were elected, which reflected the feelings of the general membership that climbing should get more

In 1941, climbing students practice their moves on "Big Rock," a glacial boulder in northeast Seattle. It's still there, on the east side of 28th Avenue Northeast about half a mile north of Northeast 56th Street. Wolf Bauer attempted to persuade the board of trustees to buy the land and build a clubhouse at the site, but the board resisted. The rock today is incorporated into a neighborhood of houses and no longer used by climbers. Photo: Lloyd Anderson collection.

respect. When the results were announced, about a dozen members resigned in protest, most of them from the committee that had ruled the lodge.

One of the new board's first acts was to dismiss the paid lodge caretakers, thereby resolving the main financial problem. The climbers group was placed under jurisdiction of the club's climbing committee, and the climbing course became officially sanctioned. It was perhaps the first of its kind in the nation.

All was well with the course as long as Bauer did most of the teaching. But there was only so much he could do before others had to be called in to help. At first, each lecturer was on his own, speaking about whatever topic he chose. This situation came to a head when one speaker expounded on his favorite libations for a club climb, even though alcohol was strictly prohibited at Mountaineers functions.

Lloyd Anderson brought things back in line. With the help of his wife, Mary, he divided the course into subjects, with qualified instructors in charge of each topic. In 1938, each instructor was required to present an outline of his topic for review by the climbing committee. The outlines were mimeographed, and each student received a copy.

In 1935, the year of the first climbing course, all the students who signed up for Bauer's instruction already were experienced climbers. But in 1939, most of the eighty who enrolled had little or no climbing experience, and in 1940, one hundred novices enrolled.

The summer outing would remain a popular activity, but the bedrock of the club's existence was shifting to climbing. The exciting tale of the 1933 attempt by Bauer and Hans Grage to forge a route up Mount Rainier's north face along Ptarmigan Ridge was one of the reasons why.

"It was a climb that neither one of us will ever forget," Bauer said in the 1934 annual. "It taught us at least one lesson, namely, that the best mountaineering is not always good mountaineering. Although the goal, Liberty Cap, was not quite reached, the North Side was conquered for the first time. . . .

"Working under cover of large projections up the right side of this chute, which was in the direct path of falling rock and ice, we crawled on hands and feet along the foot of this overhanging wall in an arcade-like undercut from the ceiling of which long icicles hung suspended.

"During this time of late afternoon, we were kept constantly on the dodge by hurtling and singing rocks."

The next year, Bauer and Jack Hossack completed the first ascent of Ptarmigan Ridge, their ice axes striking so much rock and ice that the tips bent backward and had to be pounded back into shape with rocks. The fact that they were using ice axes and other modern equipment pointed up the change in climbing philosophy.

Bold as their climb was, a few weeks later club members Ome Daiber and Will Borrow Jr., along with a friend, E. A. "Arne" Campbell, pioneered the "impossible" Liberty Ridge route on the north face of Rainier, which would become known as one of the classic climbs in American mountaineering.

Chapter 4

NO MOUNTAIN HIGH ENOUGH

Mountaineer climbers in the 1930s were well aware of their unparalleled good fortune. Only the highest Northwest peaks had been climbed, and all a young climber had to do to score a first ascent was head for the nearest blank spot on the map. Many of the mountains hadn't even been surveyed, and the climbers often went without benefit of a map. Often they explored the area first and returned later, relying on their own notes to reach a summit.

There was no method or plan for deciding upon first ascents or new routes. The process was often whimsical. For example, Borrow told in the 1935 annual how he and Daiber settled upon the Liberty Ridge route:

"One evening early in September after the adjournment of a meeting of The Mountaineers Club, Ome Daiber and I stood in the lobby admiring an unusual photograph of Mount Adams. It was soon after our conversation there in which we had commented upon the great similarity of the north faces of Mount Adams and Mount Rainier that my friend related to me his seemingly fantastic scheme of climbing to the summit of Rainier by the incredible and surely impractical route up Willis Wall (Liberty Ridge).

"At first I thought he was joking and so passed his suggestion by with a remark expressing my satisfaction with this earthly life and my good health, which I earnestly expected to continue. But in a moment seeing that he was entirely serious, I eagerly agreed to make the try with him, although I had never closely studied the mountain from the north."

The winter following the conquest of Liberty Ridge, the National Park Service asked Daiber if he would help conduct a search for Delmar Fadden, a young climber who had disappeared while attempting a solo winter climb of Mount Rainier via the Emmons Glacier. Daiber eventually found Fadden's body, and the subsequent publicity helped make Daiber one of the Northwest's best-known mountaineers. After that, he was repeatedly called upon for rescues, and with Bauer and Dr. Otto Trott of the area's Ski Patrol eventually formed the Mountain Rescue Council, upon which the national model was based.

O. Phillip Dickert, Joe Halwax, George MacGowan, and Wolf Bauer on the summit of Mount Goode in 1936. Bauer proposed the climb as a test of his climbing course graduates. They succeeded where some of the Northwest's most experienced mountaineers had failed. Jack Hossack, the fifth member of the party, took the picture. Photo: O. P. Dickert collection.

In 1936, Wolf Bauer led his first climbing course graduates on a venture he felt would test their skills. The group chose 9,200-foot Mount Goode, a fortress of a mountain at the head of Lake Chelan and one of the most sought-after first ascents in the Cascades. Herman Ulrichs had written of his attempt on Goode in the 1935 *American Alpine Journal*. Several parties of experienced club members representing the best in the Northwest, including Norval Grigg and Art Winder, had been thwarted by a particularly tricky chimney near the summit.

Among the graduates who accompanied Bauer were O. Phillip Dickert, Jack Hossack, Joe Halwax, and George MacGowan. All would go on to become familiar names in Northwest climbing.

Nothing looked very promising for this climb at the outset. The weather was wet and bleak. And on the ferry ride up Lake Chelan to the village of Stehekin, they discovered a pile of climbing equipment aboard and learned that it belonged to two Canadian climbers who also were attempting the first ascent of Goode, via the northeast side. But Bauer had had the foresight to call ahead, and the local hostelry manager was waiting for them at Stehekin with a truck. They were whisked the sixteen miles up the Stehekin River to the trailhead as soon as the boat docked, giving them a head start.

Bauer was first to reach the narrow chimney just below the summit that had stopped so many climbers before him. MacGowan wrote of that climb in the 1936 annual:

"The rear wall of the chimney sloped back at an angle of 50 to 75 degrees, and was covered with ice and snow. The side walls were also verglassed, making friction climbing impossible. Wolf worked his way up, driving pitons wherever possible, having considerable trouble making them hold in the ice-filled cracks. . . . In due course the entire party arrived at the top of the chimney, which was about 150 feet high and ended in an overhang.

"The right wall was vertical for 100 feet, and the left six or seven, slanting back to a ledge 30 feet higher. With some difficulty Wolf stemmed up between the walls, here about five feet apart, crossed and scrambled to the ledge above, where he drove a piton, to belay the remainder of the party to his side. Here we thought our difficulties were over, as the ledge led to the left in a most promising manner, but on exploring we found it ran onto the face of the cliff and we were forced to return to our original position on the ledge.

"Thirty feet higher, a break in the ridge looked like a probable solution to our difficulty, and while dubiously realizing that the first man would have very little protection, Wolf spied a crack in the granite ten feet above. The second flip of the rope caught, and ascending with prusik knots, he found himself on a narrow sloping slab with no close holds. With considerable effort he was able to drive a piton far enough to his right to protect himself until he worked over to where a finger traverse was possible.

"A few anxious moments and he was on the ridge announcing that the way was clear to the summit."

At that point, Bauer and Hossack couldn't resist a practical joke. They scrambled to the top and built a small cairn, then announced to the others that the boys from Canada had beaten them to the summit. The others were forlorn until they went looking for the summit register that would surely have been left behind and the joke was revealed. The Canadian climbers never made it.

Another example of Mountaineers skill

came in 1939, when George MacGowan and Jack Hossack climbed the northeast couloir of the Grand Teton one day during a summer outing. They had intended to rest up that day while another group climbed nearby Mount Owen, but they grew restless and headed up the Teton Glacier just to see what it looked like. Leaving the glacier, they came to a steep couloir of water-worn rock that shot high up into the Grand. The temptation was too great, and without ropes or other equipment, they dashed up it so quickly that they were on the summit before the other party reached the top of Owen. A ranger later informed them that they had accomplished the first ascent of the northeast couloir route.

Hossack would later say that he didn't find the climb particularly difficult after his Mountaineers training.

Following that, first ascents by Mountaineers came so fast they were almost too numerous to keep track of. Nobody kept a running tally, and it's difficult to determine just how many first ascents can be credited to club members.

In 1938, Lloyd Anderson, Lyman Boyer, and Agnes Dickert made the first ascent of Blue Mountain (Gunsight Peak), a slab of sheer granite near Dome Peak in the central Cascades. Dickert earned the title of "foremost woman mountain climber" in the press for climbing sixteen peaks in one summer, and later was the first woman to climb Big Four Mountain near Silverton.

In 1939, Anderson, with Clinton Kelley and Jim Crooks, made the first ascent of Sinister Peak, near Dome Peak. Anderson, with Kelley and fifteen-year-old Fred Beckey, were the first climbers to the summit of Mount Despair. Bear's Breast Mountain was climbed by Beckey, Wayne Swift, and Joe Barto.

Ken Norden (seated center on rock) and Clint Kelley (far right) take a breather during a climb in the early 1940s. Norden was among those contributing to the first "Climber's Notebook," published in 1940. Kelley was on the first ascents of Sinister Peak and Despair in 1939. Known as an outstanding teacher and leader, Kelley served on the climbing committee in 1939– 40 and again in 1977–79, when he was still actively climbing. Photo: O. P. Dickert.

In 1941, Anderson, Tom Campbell, Lyman Boyer, and Helmy Beckey made the first ascent of South Howser Spire in British Columbia's Bugaboos.

In 1942, brothers Helmy and Fred Beckey shocked the climbing world by making the second ascent of Mount Waddington in the British Columbia Coast Range. They did this by simply hiking in and climbing the peak as if it were a nearby Cascades summit, despite earlier attempts by experienced teams in the years since the peak was first climbed in 1936. Fred Beckey, who would go on to establish one of

∽

Tom Campbell, Lloyd Anderson, Lyman Boyer, and Helmy Beckey made the first ascent of South Howser Spire in British Columbia's Bugaboos in 1941. Anderson, who with his wife, Mary, founded Recreational Equipment Inc., was perhaps the top Northwest climber of the 1930s and early 1940s, scaling over five hundred peaks through the 1950s and 1960s, and scoring numerous first ascents in the Cascades, including Spire, Damnation, and Blue (Gunsight Peak) in 1938; Sinister, Blizzard, and Despair in 1939; and Forbidden, Ten Peak, and Dorado Needle in 1940. Anderson was also a leading organizer of the early years of the climbing course. Boyer accompanied Anderson and Agnes Dickert on the Blue ascent. Beckey, who was also on the first ascent of Forbidden, and his brother, Fred, shocked the climbing world in 1942, when, as still teenagers (ages seventeen and nineteen), they made the second ascent of Canada's treacherous Mount Waddington. Photo: Lloyd Anderson collection.

the world's most impressive records of first ascents, was nineteen at the time. His younger brother had just turned seventeen.

Fred Beckey would later recount: "Illness forced Erik (Larsen) to return to civilization the second day, but Helmy and I continued over the meager trail beside the raging Franklin River under 60- and 70-pound packs."

In fact, they simply left Larsen behind to make his own way back after he got sick. Such a narrow and unblinking focus on the summit would become something of a Fred Beckey trademark. If a partner wasn't up to it, that was his problem. In the years to come, Beckey would go through climbing partners faster than he went through boots and drew a reputation within the club as a guy who didn't always follow the prescribed safety rules. But Beckey's climbing exploits would become the stuff of legend. Walt Varney described one of the early climbs in the 1943 annual, an ascent on Kangaroo Ridge in the Washington Pass area of the North Cascades:

"Mushroom Tower, 8,400 feet, could have no other name because it was just that. A stratum of soft rock has worn out, leaving the dome sitting on a thick column with an overhanging pitch all around. It appears unclimbable except in one spot. And this pitch, Fred and Helmy insist, is the toughest one they have ever climbed.

"From a platform as big as a table, a three-man shoulder stand had to be used to get Fred over the 12-foot overhang onto a 10-foot slab that wasn't more than 70 degrees but had no holds or piton cracks. How Fred wormed up by traction of the palms of his hands at hip level, with legs more or less useless, is a mystery to him, too. Helmy and Walt had to climb up the fixed rope.

"On the table, we three tied ourselves so short that if Fred had slipped and missed the table, we could have held him, yet with nothing but 900 feet of air below, it would have been quite a thrill."

The newly completed (in 1939) Monitor Rock at Camp Long in West Seattle draws a crowd of climbers to practice their moves. The rock, the first man-made climbing rock in the country, constructed for use in the club's growing climbing course, was the idea of Clark E. Schurman and was later renamed in his honor. Photo: O. P. Dickert.

Descriptions of climbs in previous *Mountaineer* annuals had seldom noted the exact techniques climbers used, probably because no real technique was involved. But from this point on it became almost a matter of pride to list the techniques employed, especially in accounts by Fred Beckey.

After graduating from the University of Washington, Beckey pioneered a lifestyle that revolved around climbing, at times living out of the trunk of his car as he drove around the country in a quest for new climbs and new partners. Many climbers have followed Beckey's inspiration over the years, embracing this nomadic lifestyle for the sake of climbing.

Aside from his climbs, Beckey's crowning achievement has been his three-volume *Cascade Alpine Guide*, now published by The Mountaineers, which evolved out of his earlier book, the *Climber's Guide to the Cascade and Olympic Mountains of Washington*. The *Cascade Alpine Guide* remains indispensable for anyone climbing in the Cascades.

World War II interrupted climbing in the Northwest, but for a number of Mountaineers, military service was an opportunity to learn new techniques and associate with climbers and skiers from across the country. Some served with the 10th Mountain Division, training at Mount Rainier and in the Rockies and fighting in Italy. They not only made military contributions but managed numerous first ascents. Beckey's climbing log for 1943–44 shows climbs in Colorado, where he was stationed at Camp Hale.

With the war winding down, a special climbers outing was initiated for those unable to attend the summer outing. The first, in 1945 to the Dutch Miller Gap area, drew four women and twelve men, including Lloyd Anderson and O. Phillip Dickert. They climbed nine different peaks, including at least one first ascent, of Middle Chief Peak.

The ascents sometimes had their lighter side. Keith Rankin recounted in 1945: "Not one, but *two* courageous parties of Mountaineers were fortunate enough to gain the summit of 7,494 foot Mt. Hinman, northeast of La Bohn Gap. In an unparalleled feat of human conquest, these climbers fought their way across more than three miles of granite rock slides and trackless snow slopes—only to find that Boy Scout Troop No. 285 had reached its windswept crest before them. Cruel, cruel world!"

The era of unlimited opportunity in Northwest climbing was finished in the late 1940s, with Fred Beckey in 1948 noting matter-of-factly that exploration of the Cascade Mountains was "more or less at an end."

THE POSTWAR SURGE

The Mountaineers climbing course was now organized into basic and intermediate sections, with intermediate students serving as instructors for the basic course. There was no "advanced" course on the grounds that it might encourage students to push beyond their experience and capabilities. Numerous climb leaders were willing to sacrifice their own ambitions for the good of the course. Anderson and Bauer both admit they could have achieved many more first ascents but were primarily interested in teaching the skills to others.

Climbing course graduates were making their mark on American climbing, but no one could foresee the historical trends taking shape that would catapult club members into the foremost ranks of world climbers. Interest in mountain climbing burst open after World War II. Nearly two hundred students signed up for the Seattle climbing course in 1949, at a time when there were estimated to be only about that many active climbers in the entire state of Washington. The Everett and Tacoma branches further offered climbing courses of their own.

Rock climbing practices were held at man-made Monitor Rock (later renamed Schurman Rock) in West Seattle's Camp Long and on Little Si peak near North Bend. More serious instruction was given at Tumwater Canyon near Leavenworth. Snow practices took place at Guye Peak and Mount Kendall in Commonwealth Basin near Snoqualmie Pass.

Students in the Basic Climbing course in the 1950s use a sand and gravel pit near Issaquah to simulate snow conditions while practicing self-arrest with ice axes. Since a climber could not slide down the slope with sufficient speed, the system required that someone pull on a rope as hard as possible while a self-arrest was attempted. Photo: Paul Wiseman.

Ralph Widrig and Joe Heib on The Horn in the Olympics. Making use of the new equipment that was coming out in the 1940s, they and their contemporaries achieved ascents unheard of by the previous generation of climbers. Heib made the first wide-angle pitons used in the Northwest. Photo: Chuck Allyn.

Practices in belaying, crevasse rescue, and rappelling often were held a long way from the mountains—at the Duwamish Piers in South Seattle—augmented by "real world" instruction at Nisqually Glacier on Mount Rainier. Even the sand banks at Seattle's Fort Lawton (now Discovery Park) and later a gravel pit near the town of Issaquah were enlisted for practicing ice ax arrest, since the unstable slopes could simulate loose snow.

By the 1950s, the climbing course was recognized nationally and other outdoor groups across the country were asking for information on setting up similar courses.

A watershed event during this period was publication in 1949 of Fred Beckey's *Climber's Guide to the Cascade and Olympic Mountains of* *Washington* by the American Alpine Club. Dubbed the "green book" for its cover, or "Beckey's Bible," it made use of notes submitted by Mountaineers climbers and made available by the climbing committee. Among the first mountaineering guidebooks in the nation, it codified Cascade and Olympic climbs and took

Pete Schoening, Gib Reynolds, Dick McGowan, and Bill Niendorff at the mouth of the Malaspina Glacier at the conclusion of their 1952 King Peak–Yukon Expedition in Canada, which included a first ascent of Mount Augusta and the second ascent of King Peak via a new route from King Col. Schoening is perhaps best known in climbing lore for "The Belay," in which he single-handedly held six falling climbers at 25,000 feet on K2 in the Himalayas in 1953. In 1958 he and a partner became the first Americans to make a first ascent of an 8,000-meter peak, Gasherbrum I (Hidden Peak). McGowan went on to climb all over the world, was chief guide on Mount Rainier from 1956 to 1965, founded the Alpine Hut chain of outdoor stores and the gear manufacturer Mountain Products, and for a time was owner of the Berkeley, California–based trekking company Mountain Travel. Photo: Pete Schoening collection.*

some of the unknowns out of mountain trips.

As the old era of Northwest climbing was closing, another was opening. A new breed of climber was developing, partly as a result of the climbing course and the work of individuals who had come out of it. Hossack, Bauer, Anderson, and others had paved the way for a generation of climbers that would become respected around the world. Achievements of a difficulty that previous techniques and equipment could not overcome were soon being recorded by the Beckey brothers, Ralph Widrig, Pete Schoening, Joe Heib, Wes Grande, Dee Molenaar, and many others.

Impressive first ascents were still being done in the Cascades, but in the 1950s members of the club began turning their interests farther afield. For example, the King Peak–Yukon Expedition of 1952 saw five members of The Mountaineers in a party of eight making the first ascent of 14,070-foot Mount Augusta, as well as the second ascent of King Peak.

In 1964, a Mountaineers trip to Mount McKinley, led by Alvin Randall, placed fifteen club members on the summit. It was the most ambitious expedition ever sponsored by The Mountaineers and recorded a lengthy and unusual list of firsts for the peak. With eighteen members in all, including two husband-and-wife teams, it was the second-largest American climbing expedition on record at the time and the largest single group to ever attempt McKinley. It had the largest number of women ever to reach the summit in one party (three), and included the first African American (Charles Crenchaw) to climb the mountain.

Randall returned to Alaska four years later as leader of an American–Japanese joint expedition that achieved a number of first ascents in the Wrangell Range.

The Mountaineers expedition to Mount McKinley in 1964 achieved a number of firsts, including the first African American to reach the summit. On top are Charles Crenchaw, Frances Randall, and Alvin Randall. Al led the expedition, which placed fifteen club members on the summit. Photo: Charles De Hart, The Mountaineer *annual, 1965.*

Right: Joan Firey descends from McMillan Cirque, completing the Elephant Butte High Route and Bowling Alley Traverse in the North Cascades in 1974. She was among the women climbers who left their mark around the world and was a member of the all-woman expedition that successfully climbed Annapurna in 1978. Photo: Dave Knudson.

Among other notable Mountaineers, Lowell Skoog became known for his winter climbs in the Cascades, among them the first winter ascents of Bonanza Peak and Mount Formidable.

Mountaineers women increasingly left their mark on climbing. In 1978, Joan Firey was a member of the all-woman Annapurna I expedition. Marcia Hanson, club president in 1996–97, led all-women Mountaineers expeditions to Mount McKinley in 1989 and 1990. Susan Price, who took the basic and intermediate courses in the 1980s, turned professional climber in 1989 and became top-ranked by the American Sport Climbing Federation. Judy Waller was the first woman to climb Mount Rainier's Liberty Ridge and Mount Logan in Canada's Yukon Territory.

ON TOP OF THE WORLD

The training from the climbing course and the experience of ascents in the Cascades and Olympics enabled individual Mountaineers to reach some of the greatest heights in world climbing.

In 1953, club members Pete Schoening, Dee Molenaar, and Bob Craig were part of a party attempting the first ascent of the world's second-highest peak, K2 in Asia's Karakoram Range.

"Given a break in the weather, we were confident that the summit could be reached," Schoening wrote in the 1953 *Mountaineer* annual. "Then the Monsoon hit K2 with full force and almost unbelievable intensity. The wind and blowing snow raged on, and after 10 days at this highest camp (25,500 feet), during which time one member became ill, we started down. This seemed to be the only hope for survival. Thus, another expedition had failed to reach K2's 28,250 foot summit."

What Schoening neglected to mention was his involvement in one of the most storied episodes in mountaineering history, when he stopped the fall of six companions and saved all their lives. While descending after the summit attempt, Schoening, Molenaar, and two others were lowering team member Art Gilkey, who was dying of thrombophlebitis, toward base camp in a makeshift litter. Schoening, who was tied to Gilkey's litter, was belaying the litter from behind a large rock, with the rope wrapped around his ice ax and his waist, when George Bell slipped and fell, pulling the others off their feet. Their rope became tangled with that of a two-man team, and they all went down, with the exception of Schoening.

Somehow, Schoening managed to hold all six climbers. He later described the belay as a mixture of skill and luck. But any Mountaineer who has ever practiced an ice ax belay since then can't help but be reminded of his feat.

In 1955, an American expedition led by Norman Dyrenfurth that attempted 27,890-foot Lhotse in the Himalayas included Mountaineers members Fred Beckey and Dick McGowan. Both men were sponsored and received limited funding from the newly formed expedition committee of The Mountaineers. Weather conditions forced the team off Lhotse, but it succeeded on 21,500-foot Langcha, which became the first Nepalese peak to be climbed by Americans.

In his report in the 1955 annual, McGowan noted that the trip showed off the superiority of mountaineering clothing and sleeping bags designed in the Northwest.

"Most of the equipment used during the course of the expedition was manufactured in Europe. The Europeans used acryl-lined pants, jackets and sleeping bags, with poor results. It was no substitute for down insulation. Fortunately, [George] Bell, Beckey and I used special down articles designed by climbers in Seattle

Pete Schoening demonstrates crack climbing on House Tower in the Enchantments in 1950. Schoening was still climbing in 1996 at age sixty-nine, when he attempted to become the oldest person to reach the summit of Mount Everest. Photo: Ira Spring.

and manufactured by Eddie Bauer Inc. The garments were exceptionally durable and warm. The Europeans admitted our down clothing was superior to anything they had seen or used."

Americans Pete Schoening and Andy Kauffman achieved a goal of climbers throughout the world when in 1958 they made the first ascent of 26,470-foot Hidden Peak (Gasherbrum I) in the Karakoram Range. They became the first and only Americans ever to achieve the first ascent of an 8,000-meter peak.

Dick McGowan was a member of the American Pakistan Karakoram Expedition that reached the summit of 25,660-foot Masherbrum in 1960. But McGowan's personal effort was cut short at 24,000 feet when he was caught in an avalanche, inhaled snow, and froze portions of his lungs. McGowan was chief guide from 1956 to 1965 at Mount Rainier, where he and fellow

guide Gil Blinn one day went from road's end at Paradise to the summit crater rim and back in an astonishing six hours and forty-one minutes, a speed record that lasted for many years.

☙

Right: Maynard Miller and Dee Molenaar (foreground) at the finish of the 1946 Mount St. Elias Expedition. Besides making countless climbs in the Cascades, Olympics, Rockies, and the Selkirks of Canada, Miller participated in numerous worldwide expeditions ranging from the 1940 expedition to the Fairweather Range of southeast Alaska to geological surveys in the Himalayas. Over the last fifty years he has gained renown for his scientific studies of the relationship between glaciers and worldwide climate trends. A geologist, artist, author, and cartographer, Molenaar has climbed throughout the United States as well as in the Alps, New Zealand, and Antarctica. He participated in major expeditions to K2 (Himalayas) in 1953 and Mount Kennedy (Yukon Territory, Canada) in 1965. His book The Challenge of Rainier is the definitive work on the mountain's climbing history. Both men are honorary members of The Mountaineers. Miller is a member of the Tacoma branch and Molenaar of the Olympia branch. Photo: Dee Molenaar collection.

Dick McGowan, Tom Miller, Tim Kelley, and Franz Mohling on the beach at Yakutat Bay after their first ascent of Alaska's Mount Cook in August 1953. Following World War II, members of The Mountaineers began to expand their climbing activities far beyond the Pacific Northwest. Miller was on the second Ptarmigan Traverse in Washington's Cascades (1953) and climbed new routes on Formidable, Johannesburg, and Torment. For many years he was a leading force on the literary fund committee (which grew to become Mountaineers Books), and his dramatic black-and-white photos were featured in the book The North Cascades, *published in 1964 to publicize the struggle to create North Cascades National Park.*
Photo: John Merriman.

The most famous of international achievements by Mountaineers members came in 1963 when Jim Whittaker became the first American to stand on top of Mount Everest. Another member, Barry Bishop of Washington, D.C., was also among the six climbers who reached the summit of the world's highest mountain on that expedition. Club member and glacier expert Maynard Miller was on the expedition as well.

Whittaker's account in the 1964 annual gave fellow Mountaineers a good look at what they were in for in the Himalayas:

"We had had a terrible storm and everyone was deteriorated physically. Living this high there is an oxygen problem, and you deteriorate, no matter who you are, what you eat or how you sleep, because of the lack of oxygen in the air. The food isn't oxidized and you just don't put the weight on. I had gone down from 205 to 170 pounds, and [Sherpa Nawang] Gombu from 130 pounds down to 100 pounds. We were very weak at this point, and had decided that if the weather was bad the next day we would go back down to base camp. Then the whole expedition would pull off the mountain and recuperate."

Camp VI was at 27,500 feet. "We moved very slowly at that elevation. It took us an hour the next morning to pull our boots on. It took us another hour to make enough fluid. We had a cup of hot Jell-O apiece. This was our only fluid for the next twelve hours. I had put the canteen of water in my pack with no insulation. An hour later we went to pull it out and it was solid ice, so we had no fluid the whole twelve hours.

"When Gombu and I moved out, the winds in the South Col, 1,500 feet below us, were estimated to be 80 miles an hour. The temperature was 20 below zero. Nevertheless, as the Mountaineers know, when you are on a mountain like Everest, you stick your neck out a little further than maybe you would on any other mountain. We stuck ours out, and decided to go on anyway. . . .

"About five or ten feet before the summit, I stopped and saw it sloping off the back side. I took in the rope. Gombu came up to me. I put my head against him and said, 'Gombu, you go first.' He said, 'You first, big Jim,' and I said, 'No, you first, Gombu.' He said, 'You go, big Jim.' I said, 'Gombu,' he said, 'You.' So I

took his arm and we walked the last five feet together. . . ."

In 1990 Whittaker organized the American–Soviet–Chinese International Peace Climb, in which a remarkable total of twenty representatives of the three countries reached the summit. Ascent teams were composed of three climbers, one from each nation. As an additional achievement, the expedition removed two tons of garbage from the mountain, debris that had been left by other expeditions.

Closer to home in the postwar era, club members were likewise setting foot atop or forging new routes up some of the most notable peaks in this country and Canada.

Pete Schoening led a party into the Coast Range of British Columbia in 1951 to make the first ascent of Mount Saugstad. In 1953, Tom Miller, Tim Kelley, Franz Mohling, and Dick McGowan made the first ascent of Alaska's 13,760-foot Mount Cook during an expedition to the St. Elias Range.

Don Claunch (who later changed his name to Don Gordon) in 1955 achieved a sensational first ascent of Wishbone Arête on Mount Robson in the Canadian Rockies, a route that had been tried many times before, going all the way back to Swiss guide Walter Schauffelberger's 1913 attempt. Claunch also made many first ascents in the Cascades, including the north face of Mount Maude, the Mowich face of Mount Rainier, and the south face of Cutthroat Peak. But among Mountaineers members he may be known best for his "all the way on foot" climbs in the Cascade front range, starting out and ending at his home in Seattle and not using any type of vehicle or mechanical aid for travel.

Another remarkable achievement on Mount Robson was the first ascent of its formidable north face by Dan Davis and Pat Callis in 1964. To prepare for this climb, Davis and Callis had made the first winter ascent of the sinister North Peak of Mount Index in the Cascades in 1963. Of the Mount Robson climb, Davis wrote in the 1964 annual:

"Pat Callis and I had heard a lot about the unclimbed north face of Robson from the many Seattle climbers who had either looked at it or attempted to climb it—so much that we felt compelled to have a look at it ourselves. On August 1 we left Seattle by Volkswagen for our first climbing trip in Canada.

"By the time we reached the major rock band, it had become light and we were finally able to see just how steep and exposed the face was. It seemed rather awe-inspiring at the time. Unfortunately, in this area we found ourselves climbing on loose, insecure powder snow over glare ice. From here to the Emperor Ridge, the snow would never hold our weight. Whenever we stepped on it, it gave way until our feet were resting on the ice beneath. We put on crampons at this point, and belayed continuously.

"Usually to set up a belay we had to scoop out several square feet of loose snow in order to stand on the solid ice and to anchor ourselves with ice pitons. We belayed this way for twelve 150-foot rope lengths before reaching Emperor Ridge. We were climbing straight up, with the only deviations being slight ones to either side when we thought we could find better snow conditions there.

"On one of the last moves on the face, Pat actually imbedded the picket vertically with his hammer, climbed up on it, and then used it for a foothold to climb farther. For the largest part of the upper face we climbed on all fours as much as the angle of the face would permit. The anticipated rock bands on the upper face

presented no problems at all, due to the heavy snow on the face."

To round out these world conquests, in 1966 Pete Schoening participated in the first American Antarctic climbing expedition, which was the first to reach the highest point of that continent, the 16,864-foot Vinson Massif.

Neil Jacques and Bob Latz on the Peshastin Pinnacles in 1966, getting ready to climb Grand Central Tower. Latz was climbing chairman in 1959 and club president in 1961– 63, but he is perhaps best remembered by his peers for his frugality and unwavering devotion to Army surplus gear and clothing. Photo: Keith Gunnar.

Dan Davis on the North Peak of Mount Index during the first winter ascent of the peak in January 1963. He was accompanied by Pat Callis. Davis is one of the most prolific climbers in the Northwest. Between 1959 and 1983 he climbed 429 different routes on 261 peaks for a total of 571 climbs, including the first ascent of the north face of Mount Robson in 1964 (also with Callis) and a number of other significant winter ascents. He has been leading Mountaineers club climbs from 1961 to the present. Photo: Pat Callis.

⚭

Fred Beckey, Don (Claunch) Gordon, and Ed Cooper on their way to attempt the 3,500-foot north face of Mount Baring in July 1959. The vertical north face had frustrated countless other parties and taken at least one life. Beckey had to descend early to make it back to work on time, but Gordon and Cooper continued on to complete the first ascent. Beckey and Cooper, climbing companions for quite a while, were soon competing for first ascents. Cooper established a name for himself with his big wall climbs in the Cascades and the Bugaboos (British Columbia), on the Grand Wall of Squamish Chief (B.C.) in 1961, and the Dihedral Wall of El Capitan in Yosemite in 1962. He went on to become a prolific, well-known climbing and outdoor photographer. Gordon had previously completed a first ascent of the Wishbone Arête on Mount Robson as well as a number of difficult firsts on faces of Mount Rainier. Photo: Ed Cooper.

Right: Victor Josendal negotiates the Fuhrer Finger at about 13,000 feet on Mount Rainier in 1959. Among his accomplishments was a first ascent of Mount Augusta on the King Peak–Yukon Expedition of 1952. On the 1961 climber's outing to the St. Elias Range in Canada's Yukon Territory, he led two successful first ascents of unnamed peaks. Photo: Keith Gunnar.

Below: The Bulgers, a guerrilla-climbing offshoot of The Mountaineers, were known for completing climbs of the one hundred highest peaks in Washington State and for their exploratory winter climbs. On the summit of Bedal Peak in 1983: Mary Jo Gibbs and Bette Felton (seated), Mike Bialos, Bob Tillotson, Silas Wild,* Bruce Gibbs, Russ Kroeker,* and John Roper (standing). Photo: John Roper.

John Klos shows his rock-climbing skills for photographer Ira Spring on Mount Shuksan in the 1950s. Klos, climbing committee chairman in 1945, is known as a great teacher and friend of beginner climbers and continues to climb and lead hikes today. Photo: Ira Spring.

⚬

Above: Lowell Skoog, shown on Mount Shuksan in 1994, has always enjoyed what he calls "the mystery of the unknown." With a variety of partners, but chiefly with his brother Carl, he pioneered about three hundred miles of high-route ski traverses in the Cascades and Olympics, including the Isolation Traverse (Snowfield to Eldorado) in 1983; the first ski traverse of the Picket Range in 1985; the Thunder High Route (Rainy Pass to Eldorado) in 1987; and the first one-day ski crossing of the Ptarmigan Traverse in 1988. He also completed the first winter ascents of Bonanza in 1979, Formidable and the Price Glacier on Shuksan in 1981, and Triumph and Despair in 1986. Photo: Lowell Skoog collection.

Left and Above: Helen Thayer, at age fifty, became the first woman to journey solo to the magnetic North Pole. At fifty-six, with husband Bill, sixty-six, she kayaked 1,200 miles of the Amazon River basin and, at fifty-nine, became the first woman to walk 1,400 miles across the Sahara Desert. In 1997, at sixty, she attempted a solo trek to the South Pole, but a leg injury from a sled accident ended that bid 200 miles into the 800-mile journey. Photos: Helen Thayer collection.

Chapter 5

WINTER WONDERLAND

Organized alpine skiing in Western Washington can be traced back to 1912, when Olive Rand brought a pair of skis on a Mountaineers trip to Mount Rainier. That January outing by the Tacoma branch made history as Rand became the first person to reach Longmire from the park boundary on a pair of the "wooden boards."

Skis caught on fast. Norm Engle and Thor Bisgaard, both of the Tacoma branch, began making ski trips to Paradise Valley in 1914, and by 1916 the club was mounting annual trips to the newly completed Paradise Inn, which The Mountaineers was allowed to rent for its exclusive use for five days each winter.

At that time, getting to Paradise was no easy matter. Seattle Mountaineers started the trip by lugging their skis and snowshoes to the ferry dock for a morning boat ride to Tacoma. From there, groups of sometimes 180 or more went by steam train to Ashford, then hiked the ten miles or so to Longmire from the end of the rail line. They spent the first night at Longmire Inn, and the next day the skiers and snowshoers hiked up to Paradise, which in heavy snow could be a tough slog. There they remained for

several days, the skiers repeatedly climbing the slopes for the ride down.

This early, rugged skiing brought Mountaineers winter activities to life. No longer were members forced to choose between local walks at low elevations or staying indoors until the snow melted. Robert Hayes described the impact of skiing, in the 1933 annual:

"Snoqualmie Pass a few years ago was almost as remote and mysterious in winter as is Little America [Antarctica] today. It was not only an event but an actual achievement for anyone outside of the initiated to visit the summit in winter months.

"Longmire afforded the more venturesome facilities for tobogganing and snowshoeing, and those hardier souls who secured skis and thereby risked their limbs were the source of curiosity and amusement to onlookers."

Getting information about skiing was a challenge in the 1920s. Most of the equipment came from Europe, and European catalogs were in great demand as club members surveyed the latest gear and tried to figure out how it was supposed to be used. This equipment and apparel were then tried by Northwest skiers, who

Participants line up for the Women's Ski Race at Snoqualmie Lodge in 1919. The race was the precursor of numerous other events for women at a time when the public was just beginning to become aware of skiing. Photo: C. G. Morrison, Special Collections, University of Washington Libraries, neg. no. 18138.

debated how well it held up to local conditions.

Seattle retailer Piper & Taft advertised skis in the *Mountaineer* annual as early as 1912, but it took other businesses a few more years to catch on. In 1920, Kimball Gun Store in Tacoma advertised skis in the annual. And in 1922 Seattle Tent & Awning opened the OutDoor Store, featuring "Northland skis and those put out by Swedish Importing Co. in 6 ft. to 8 ft. lengths, in pine, ash and hickory."

Outfitter and equipment retailer Eddie Bauer (no relation to Wolf Bauer) attended a Mountaineers winter outing in early 1921 and recognized the sales opportunities. By 1928, the Eddie Bauer store in downtown Seattle was stocking a full line of skis imported from Europe. And by 1933, Eddie Bauer Inc. had embarked on some light manufacturing of skis, as had other Northwest firms, including Anderson & Thompson Ski Company of Seattle.

Although club members became knowledgeable about skiing, the public wasn't so well informed. Wolf Bauer had emigrated to Seattle in 1925 from Bavaria, where skiing was part of everyday life. But most people in Seattle at that time had never even seen a pair of skis. Bauer recalls his excitement when in that same year he was invited to go on a ski trip by his Scoutmaster, Harry Higman.

"Will I ever forget that first invitation to come along on a ski outing to Stampede Pass?" Bauer recounts in the 1963 annual. "Loaded with skis and rucksack, I proceeded to board the streetcar to King Street station for my first American ski holiday. There seemed to be, however, a little matter of reaching that train in time, for the Seattle transit system, it became evident, had not yet briefed its conductors on the shape of things to come. Poking my evil-smelling slats through the streetcar door at the conductor, I was bluntly informed that the system was not in the lumber-hauling business, and that whatever it was that I was carrying did not come under 'personal and reasonable luggage.' "

An elderly Swede came to Bauer's rescue, explaining to the conductor that the two long sticks the youth was carrying were in fact sporting equipment. The conductor gave way in the face of their combined Swedish and Teutonic accents, and Bauer made it onto the streetcar. Like other Europeans, he helped introduce a sport that would quickly consume every winter weekend for outdoor enthusiasts in the Cascades.

The long Norwegian skis used in the early days were soon replaced by the broader, shorter models popularly known in Switzerland as slalom skis. In 1925, the bindings advertised by the OutDoor Store were nothing more than a series of straps, adjusted so the user could kneel on the skis. Inability to do so was considered unsafe. Clothing was whatever one happened to have. Special ski pants came increasingly into use during the 1930s, though some skiers preferred the stylishness of knickers and golf stockings.

University Book Store advertised a complete line of equipment in 1932. Boots were $6.00, skis were $3.50, ski jackets $3.95, bindings $3.50 to $4.50, Norwegian bamboo poles $2.25, and wax 35 cents. In 1933, the Outing Equipment Company advertised skis "new and used . . . 1,000 pairs to choose from."

By 1933, skiers could purchase the latest downhill cable bindings, which allowed for both touring and downhill skiing. Metal edges were becoming popular in Europe, but most skiers in the Northwest considered them for experts only since they required delicate skill in edging.

In lieu of ski boots, climbing boots were often used for skiing, as were work boots. But by 1935 ski boots—with rugged soles, grooved heels, and square toes—were available. These new boots were of particular interest to women because they came in widths suited to them, and women no longer had to make do with ill-fitting men's sizes.

Proper waxing could spell the difference between joy and misery on skis. A properly waxed

Lars Lovseth (seated) drives caulks into the soles of his boots during the 1924 outing to Mount Rainier. The caulks or "nails" were screwed or hammered into the leather for extra traction on rocks, logs, ice, and snow. Photo: Mable V. Nash, Special Collections, University of Washington Libraries, neg. no. 18132.

ski glides smoothly through the snow but adheres sufficiently to allow the skier to walk uphill. As Wolf Bauer explained, "Those of us who could read Scandinavian [languages] or German had the inside track with waxing instructions on the early cans." Canvas climbing socks for skis, forerunner of modern climbing skins, came into use in the mid-1930s to help keep skis from sliding backward on an uphill trek.

SKIING TAKES OFF

By the late 1920s, organized skiing in Western Washington centered on jumping contests and general skiing. Jumping events were held in Leavenworth and Cle Elum and at Snoqualmie Pass. Many Mountaineers, however, concentrated on being able to survive ski trips to nearby mountains, using turning and braking techniques for the descent.

Instruction in those days was not an organized effort. If you had a friend with a little skill at skiing, you could get some pointers. Within The Mountaineers, more advanced skiers helped novices raise their skills to those necessary for ski trips.

Technique in the early 1920s generally consisted of pointing the skis downhill and shoving off—straight back down to where you started. If you managed to stay on your feet, your technique was adequate. The turn known as the stem christiania, which was being adopted across Europe, was not yet widely used in the Cascades. The advent of slalom skiing at the 1932 Olympic Games at Lake Placid, New York, changed all that, as proper technique began to be pursued as an end in itself.

Skiing got bigger and bigger within The Mountaineers. A committee set up in 1927, looking for a way to alleviate the crush at Snoqualmie Lodge from winter sports enthusiasts, developed the Meany Ski Hut near Stampede Pass. The hut about eighteen miles east of Snoqualmie Pass was the first of the club's cabins devoted specifically to skiing.

The ski committee also supervised races, arranged for instruction, and raised the general standard of skiing among members—and of the public as well. It developed a series of tests similar to those used in Europe to help classify skiers and promote systematic learning.

When the tests began in 1929, you could win a third-class rating by showing a broad range of beginner skills, including proper kick turns, both uphill and downhill; level running with the use of ski poles; and ascent of a fairly steep slope by sidestepping, half-sidestepping, and herring-boning. You also had to demonstrate two continuous stem turns, both right and left, on a gentle slope at slow speed, plus a right and left telemark turn, coming to a stop from a direct descent at slow speed. And there was more: a climb of at least five hundred vertical feet in an hour or less, with a return to the starting point within fifteen minutes, and a cross-country trip of at least four miles.

The first-class requirements were tougher, of course: at least four continuous stem christianias on a steep slope at high speed, at least four successive jump turns at fair speed, a climb of two thousand vertical feet in ninety minutes with a return time of twenty-five minutes, and a cross-country trip of eighteen miles in a day.

The highway over Snoqualmie Pass was kept open for the first time during the winter of 1930–31, creating unprecedented access. In the mid-1930s the Seattle Parks Department cleared a small patch of trees, creating Municipal Hill, and allowed a concessionaire to build a small rope tow. Skiers flocked to the hill. It was the beginning of the commercial ski areas at Snoqualmie Pass.

OFF TO THE RACES

The Mountaineers program today emphasizes backcountry skiing and ski mountaineering, but in the 1930s the focus was on competition and racing. New skiers fresh off the practice slopes and cross-country trips wanted to put their skills to the test.

As early as 1922, a trophy was offered for competition among women. And in 1923 the Harper Novice Cup was added for men. By 1929 and 1930, eight trophies were being awarded to the winners of different events.

Starting out the winter racing season from the mid-1920s and into the 1930s was the women's race. It covered about two miles, starting from Snoqualmie Lodge and heading toward Snoqualmie Pass, then swinging toward the Beaver Lake trail and back to the starting point. A men's race followed somewhat the same route but was longer.

The Harper Novice Cup race came next. It became the highlight of the winter sports season, probably due to the drama and comedy in a mass of beginning skiers trying to negotiate a race course. As Paul Shorrock recalled in the 1963 annual: "The first time I ever skied was at Snoqualmie Lodge on Washington's Birthday, 1925. On this day I entered the Harper Novice Cup Race and won it. The competition must have been as unskilled as I was."

Next in the season came the slalom and downhill races, with trophies provided by Robert Hayes and W. J. "Bill" Maxwell. Both courses were run on Meany Hill, next to Meany Ski Hut, and had the aim of promoting efficiency in turns on the slalom course and speed and skill in downhill running.

The Mountaineers Skiers group was organized in 1935 to handle instruction and testing and to develop new ski areas. A series of classes that began in October was opened to the public and drew more than one hundred participants. In the ten years since Wolf Bauer had trouble getting his skis on the streetcar, the sport had gained wide recognition.

In 1936, Andy Anderson wrote in the *Mountaineer* annual: "Skiing has such a firm grip on the public that we, who broke the trail,

∞

Known as "Wild Bill" Maxwell for his energetic skiing technique, William J. Maxwell (shown here in 1927) was an early proponent of ski racing. Photo: W. J. Maxwell Collection, Special Collections, University of Washington Libraries, neg. no. 18133.

The winners of the first Ski Patrol race were Hans-Otto Giese, Fred Ball, and Andy Anderson. The race was run in teams from Snoqualmie Lodge to Meany Ski Hut, a distance of about eighteen miles.
Photo: W. J. Maxwell Collection, Special Collections, University of Washington Libraries, neg. no. 18134.

view with unbelieving eyes things we dreamed of but hardly hoped to see, until our worn old skis and our moth-eaten Bergens [packs] were only objects to gaze at in fond remembrance."

Anderson and Norval Grigg are credited with dreaming up the Patrol Race. This strange and grueling ski race through the mountains became a premier winter event in Washington State and was open to public participation.

The race route was the eighteen miles between Snoqualmie Lodge and Meany Ski Hut—a route that was the subject of much discussion even before the hut was dedicated in November 1928. In February of that year, a Mountaineers scouting party consisting of Rudy Amsler, Andy Anderson, Bill Maxwell, Bill Marzolf, Alex Fox, and Lars Lovseth left the

lodge to explore the way, intending to join a winter outing taking place at Stampede Pass.

This first reconnaissance added considerable mystery to the race that was to follow, since even these experts had difficulty negotiating the route. The course that was finally adopted left Snoqualmie Lodge at about 3,200 feet, climbed via Olallie Meadows to 4,500 feet on the northeast side of Tinkham Peak, dropped down to Mirror Lake at 4,200 feet and on down to Yakima Pass at 3,500 feet, then up to the head of Meadow Creek at 3,700 feet, down Meadow Creek to the junction of Dandy Creek at 3,000 feet, back up to Dandy Pass at 3,700 feet, and down to Meany Hut at 2,900 feet.

The scouting party deviated from this route, choosing to go past Stirrup Lake, and didn't reach Dandy Pass until late afternoon. The men couldn't agree on which way to go from there.

With the uncertainty and approaching night, they decided to stop right where they were. They enlarged a hole in the snow around a dead snag, lining the bottom with boughs and making a bench around the outside so they could sit or lie. Then they set fire to the snag—with such success that they were alternately driven out of the hole by the heat and back in by the cold. It was not a restful night. At first light, the group continued down toward Stampede Pass and joined the worried outing members in time for breakfast.

The Patrol Race owes its inspiration to Norwegian army maneuvers in which a unit such as a machine gun team is dispatched to a certain point, each member carrying a piece of the equipment and all arriving together. In the annual Patrol Race, teams started about ten minutes apart, and the three members in each team were required to cross the finish line within one minute of each other. Each team had to carry an ax, compass, first-aid equipment, candles, a contour map, fifty feet of quarter-inch rope, emergency rations, flashlight, matches, snow glasses, and clothing.

Though ten pounds was the minimum pack weight required, packs typically weighed fifteen to twenty pounds, since most skiers carried additional items such as food, ski wax, extra ski tips, and repair parts for bindings. Average time for the trip was between five and six hours.

"The night preceding one of these grueling tests would be a scene of much activity, speculation and secret planning at the old [Snoqualmie] lodge," Paul Shorrock wrote in the 1956 annual. "Theories on everything from ski wax to fad diets were discussed with passionate partisanship. There were those who asserted that you raced on the dinner you ate the night

before, and according to them, the less breakfast eaten, the better. Those of the hearty breakfast school of thought brought their own lamb chops, steaks, or whatever they figured would best energize them for the long trek.

"Most of the participants took the whole thing very seriously and even went into the contest with intense competitiveness, but I remember one year when three men from another club entered who knew little about skiing and cared less about winning. They signed in just for the fun of the trip across, and no three men ever had a better time."

Excitement always ran high at the finish line, Shorrock said. "To watch the men at the end of an 18-mile race over the roughest kind of terrain, their legs all numb from fatigue, try to run down the steep lane at Meany and cross the finish line in some kind of an upright position filled the audience with suspense, sympathy and admiration."

The Patrol Race was discontinued in 1941 due to waning public interest. By that time, there were rope tows and other attractive options on the slopes, and the demands of the race made it less appealing to recreational skiers.

But the Patrol Race route from Snoqualmie Lodge to Meany Hut continued to hold its fascination for Mountaineers. "It was quite a satisfaction suddenly to appear on the lane at Martin (near Meany Hut) complete with pack and to answer the question, 'Where did you come from?' by saying, 'Oh, we've just come from the lodge,'" Fred Ball recounted in the 1963 annual.

Another popular event, the Silver Skis race, was the brainchild of Mountaineers member Hans-Otto Giese. He suggested it to Royal Brougham, a sportswriter for the Seattle *Post-Intelligencer*, and it caught Brougham's fancy as a way of proving to the world that the Northwest offered great skiing. Though the club had no official connection with the Silver Skis competition, many of the racers over the years were Mountaineers.

The race was laid out on a more or less straight course down Mount Rainier's Muir Snowfield, from Camp Muir to Paradise, a distance of some four miles with a drop of about forty-five hundred feet. Begun in April 1934, the race typically saw sixty to eighty participants start and forty or so finish, with the rest limping in as best they could.

Though ski race slopes were being groomed in Europe by 1934, the concept was almost unheard of in the Northwest and the race crossed whatever snow Rainier had to offer—starting near the edge of the Cowlitz Glacier and plunging down the snowfield to Panorama Point and Paradise.

The first Silver Skis championship was a spectacle never seen before or probably since. Sixty skiers, including a batch of Mountaineers, lined up and started together at the sound of a shotgun, an arrangement guaranteed to cause chaos and confusion. Moreover, just a few hundred yards from the start the racers were funnelled into a chute. It was the first of only two gates on the course, the other one being way below at Panorama Point. The eventual winner, Don Fraser, made it through this first chute along with a few others, but the rest of the pack merged into a swirling mass of arms, legs, poles, skis, and snow.

"We all funnelled for that first gate and hit this wind slab," Wolf Bauer recalled for the *Post-Intelligencer* in 1994. "It was like a washboard, and at 50 mph or so, the fastest part of the race, we were out of control. I did a complete somersault and lost both of my poles."

Temperatures ranged from a skiable twenty-six degrees at Camp Muir to a slushy forty-six at Paradise, so the skiing got progressively slower and tougher as the contestants neared the finish line. Bauer finished fifth, handicapped by the lack of poles. Don Fraser's winning time was ten minutes, forty-nine seconds.

Skier Art Wilson also recalled that first race: "They lined us all up . . . and shot the starting gun. We were too close together and I decided to wait until the crowd cleared a little. As I stood there, the starter called to me, 'If you are going to be in this race, you'd better start now.' So I did, coming in 15th. But I was glad I had not pushed off with the mob. There were a number of collisions. . . . Ben Thompson broke his jaw, and Forrie Farr his ankle. Wolf Bauer lost his poles in the melee, and I am convinced it cost him first place."

The Silver Skis race was canceled after the 1940 run, when Sigurd Hall, the first man to make it to the top of Mount Rainier on skis, was killed during the race when he ran into fog and plowed headfirst at high speed into rocks above Panorama Point.

Earlier, as The Mountaineers became more involved in ski events, the club had decided to sponsor a team that might train for national or international competition. The skiers got uniforms that team member Wolf Bauer described as "natty sweaters with insignias that even the most nearsighted judge could not fail to identify a mile away." The emblem consisted of the letter M formed by two snow-clad peaks against an oval background of blue sky and green mountains.

In 1935, the national downhill and slalom championships and Olympic trials were held at Paradise. Entries were limited, and no Mountaineers competed, but they were nevertheless humbled as they watched the Austrian and Dartmouth University teams. Northwest skiers went into the trials believing they could hold their own with anyone, but came away with an

The Mountaineers Ski Team at Mount Baker in the mid-1930s: Scott Osborn, Wolf Bauer, Bill Miller, Tim Hill, and Don Blair (in front). Photo: Robert H. Hayes, The Mountaineer *annual, 1936.*

awareness that the rest of the world had developed much better techniques.

A high point of Mountaineers skiing came in 1948 when Janette Burr won the Harriman Cup and the title of Women's National Downhill Champion. Janette was the daughter of longtime skier and climber Wally Burr and had honed her skills in club races at Meany Ski Hut. Meany skiers even had an informal group called the B Club, meaning "been beaten by Burr."

TO THE TOP ON SKIS

"Finding that skiing on small hills was extremely pleasant and that higher hills were even more alluring, our ambition was aroused to ski as high as possible on our nearest large hill, namely Mount Rainier," Bill Maxwell wrote in the 1927 annual. These ventures were not club events, but almost all of the participants were Mountaineers.

In April 1927, Mountaineers Maxwell, Andy

Anderson, and Lester Labelle tried to ascend on skis from Glacier Basin via the Emmons Glacier on the northeast side of the mountain. Their two attempts were turned back by poor weather.

In April 1928, Maxwell and Anderson tried the same route again, along with Fred Deepest, Lars Lovseth, Walter Best, Otto Strizek, and Hans-Otto Giese. They made it up the Inter Glacier, but past Steamboat Prow the snow became progressively icier until at about 11,800 feet the skis had to be abandoned. Strizek, Giese, and Best donned crampons and walked to the summit.

Mountaineers member Sigurd Hall, a specialist in ski jumping who was new to this country from Norway, made the first successful ski ascent on July 2, 1939. He and a partner, Andy Hennig, followed the same route as previous teams. Hall was able to reach the summit without removing his skis, but Hennig found it necessary to follow on foot. Icy conditions made downhill skiing impossible, so Hall put on crampons and carried his skis back to the 12,000-foot level and skied down from there.

It wasn't until summer 1947 that skiers made a full descent of Mount Rainier on skis. After being weathered off the mountain twice that summer, the team of Cliff Schmidtke, Dave Roberts, Kermit Bengtson, and Charles Welsh made its third summit attempt via the Emmons Glacier. Above Steamboat Prow, three of the men switched to crampons, but despite the ice, Roberts continued on skis all the way to the top.

"In the meantime, several climbing parties, including our support party, had overtaken and passed us, and as we wearily made our way over Crater Rim, most of the climbers waved us farewell as they commenced their downward journey," Welsh wrote in the 1948 annual.

After a quick stop on top, the team skied down roped in pairs, each man carrying a pole in one hand and an ice ax in the other. As Welsh recalled: "The first 2,000 feet were extremely icy and were cut by two very large bergschrunds, so we moved one man per rope at a time, the stationary man giving a running ice-ax belay. This system proved to be both safe and rapid, so we soon found ourselves below the bergschrund area, headed down toward a sea of murky, yellow-tinged clouds."

The skiers passed all the foot parties on the way down, beating them to Steamboat Prow. Wet snow prevailed at the prow, but from Camp Curtis, they enjoyed a fast run down the Inter Glacier on firm snow.

SKIING THE BACKCOUNTRY

The Mountaineers unveiled its first ski mountaineering course in December 1941, coincidentally just as the United States entered World War II—and to the course organizers' amazement, one hundred people registered. Thirty-one actually completed the course, and eight fulfilled the stiff requirements for graduation.

That first course was offered through the ski committee chaired by Walter Little. The club had earlier set up a winter mountaineering course, in 1938, developed by then ski committee chairman Harry Cameron, which also included use of skis.

Following World War II, the club's emphasis on ski competition gave way to backcountry skiing. Metal edges were the norm by the late 1930s, and safety release bindings were in common use by the late 1950s. Backcountry travel skis frequently had holes drilled into each end so they could be tied together and used as an emergency toboggan. Skiers often carried spare tips with them, since the tips of the wooden skis of that era were prone to breaking. Lace-up

Left: Gary Rose, shown working on his skis in the Wallowa Mountains of Oregon in 1959, worked as a Mount Rainier guide and was an early employee at Recreational Equipment Inc. and later an executive there. He was often part of the group that accompanied the Fireys on their backcountry skiing and climbing adventures to remote parts of the Cascades and the Coast Range of Canada. Photo: Frank Fickeisen.

Below: Joe and Carla Firey on the summit of East Tillie's Tower in 1969. The Firey name probably appears in more North Cascades summit registers than any other save Fred Beckey's. Seeking out high routes in the Cascades and Canada's Coast Range, Joe and his wife, Joan, along with daughter Carla, amassed numerous first ascents. Photo: Dave Knudson.

Irene and John Meulemans at the Cashmere Crags in 1959. The Meulemans were perhaps best known
for their backcountry skiing adventures. Along with the Fireys, Stella Degenhardt, Gary Rose,
Hal Williams, and others, they routinely skied the remotest parts of the Cascades.
Usually, they were completely alone. Photo: Keith Gunnar.

leather boots were used through the 1940s, with buckle boots arriving in the late 1950s and plastic boots in the 1960s.

The Mountaineers skiers divided into two groups in 1950: the competitive ski committee, to control competition and supervise lessons for beginners, and the recreational ski committee, to conduct ski tours and the ski mountaineering course.

Much of the equipment used in the postwar era was cumbersome and heavy, often surplus Army gear. Yet this was something of a golden era for backcountry skiing. In reminiscing in 1996, Irene Meulemans noted the remarkable absence of other skiers through the 1960s.

"Mount St. Helens, Naches Peak, Camp Muir, Glacier Peak, Mount Baker—we had the wilderness all to ourselves. There were probably fewer than one hundred of us in The Mountaineers who were avid backcountry skiers, and as a result, when we skied in those areas we never saw anyone else."

Irene, her husband John, Gary Rose, Hal Williams, Joan Firey, and a few others became part of Joe Firey's small but determined group

of ski mountaineers. They kept at it year after year, skiing in the remotest parts of the Cascades, the British Columbia Coast and Interior Ranges, and the Canadian Rockies. They bagged numerous first ski ascents along the way, and Joe Firey and some of the others are still at it.

Cross-country skiing on narrower, lightweight Nordic skis became popular in the early 1970s. In 1975 a Nordic ski committee was formed, and seminars were offered on telemark turns. By this time, the club's embrace of vigorous recreational skiing of all sorts had brought the history of Northwest skiing full circle, back to where it started.

Downhill skiing, cross-country touring, backcountry skiing, and ski mountaineering, as well as snowboarding, are now among the choices for winter recreation. Much of the change in skiing can be attributed to improved techniques learned because ski lifts allow people to make as many training runs in a day as they can handle, or as many as the lift lines allow. With improved understanding of technique, better equipment, and a lot of practice time, skiers have gotten much better at their sport.

Chapter 6

AT HOME
IN THE SNOW

Any Mountaineer who likes skiing and playing in the snow has a roster of lodges to pick from for winter getaways. The club owns lodges at Snoqualmie Pass, Stevens Pass, the Mount Baker ski area, and near Stampede Pass—comfortable but rustic and unpretentious places where members and their guests find friendly accommodations at low cost.

The Snoqualmie Lodge and the Meany Ski Hut near Stampede Pass are on club-owned land, while the other two are on property leased from the U.S. Forest Service. Visiting groups are welcome, and a policy of no alcoholic beverages adds to the attraction of the lodges as places for young people and families to gather.

The club nearly ended up with five ski lodges

Linda Coleman doing a bit of first aid on Amos Hand on the 1951 summer outing. Coleman, a nurse, went on her first outing in 1911, and in forty-one years as a Mountaineer missed just two summer outings. Doctors and nurses from Seattle's Swedish Hospital, along with her Mountaineers friends, built a memorial picnic shelter near Snoqualmie Lodge in her memory. Hand, a typesetter at the Tacoma News Tribune, *was active in the Tacoma branch and a fixture on summer outings from 1922 into the 1950s. A respected climb and outing leader, he was known for his climbing feats. On the 1932 summer outing he climbed Mount Hood, Mount St. Helens twice, and Mount Adams three times. In 1933 he climbed all six of the state's major peaks—twice.*
Photo: Special Collections, University of Washington Libraries, neg. no. 18153.

after it paid for an option to build on Forest Service land at Crystal Mountain near Mount Rainier. The project never went ahead, partly because of expensive water and sewage requirements, but also because not enough volunteers were willing to step forward and take up the project.

SNOQUALMIE LODGE

Despite controversies over the old Snoqualmie Lodge as a required base for climbing activities and the lodge's drain on club finances, the building and its location proved ideal for skiing and other winter sports. There were few who didn't love the lodge for its beauty and charm.

Any remaining concerns about the lodge became suddenly moot on a hot September day in 1944. As caretaker Andy Anderson was cleaning up waste and burning it in the big fireplace, a spark made its way through the rock of the unlined chimney and set the roof on fire. Anderson climbed to the roof and began tearing away the shingles, burning his hands, but he didn't have enough water on hand to douse the fire. He was forced to stand back and watch as the lovely structure burned to the ground.

The club received twenty-four hundred dollars in insurance money for the loss, and in 1945 the board voted to abandon the Forest Service site and build a new lodge. The Mountaineers bought eighty acres adjoining the highway from Northern Pacific Railroad for eleven hundred dollars. The new site, several miles from the old, was ideal for skiing—so much so that the properties to the north and south became commercial ski areas. The lodge is just a short hike from the chairlifts.

Building the new Snoqualmie Lodge was another grand exercise in volunteerism. Among those on the building committee was Andy Anderson, who felt so bad about losing the old lodge that he became the inspiration for the volunteers, urging them on and turning out for many work parties. T. Davis Castor, building committee chairman, was a driving force behind the new lodge.

As with the original Snoqualmie Lodge, much of the lumber was milled from trees logged on the site. The logs were taken for sawing to the Preston Mill—owned by the father of member Dave Lind—and the lumber was brought back.

The source for water was a spring on the hill above the site, with gravity flow into a cedar tank that had been disassembled and brought over from the old lodge. Work parties made tables, benches, kitchen cabinets, and storage facilities. The dining tables and benches built by Wally Burr are still in use. The only person hired during the project was a man who constructed the footing for the chimney.

Evelyn MacDonald noted that any man or woman who knew how to use a hammer or other tool was put to work. Joe Appa, a stonemason from Switzerland, heard about the project from members Jack and Catherine Crabill, and he visited one weekend out of curiosity. He got hooked. Appa kept coming, using his weekends to build the intricate fireplace facing, cutting the stone by hand with hammer and chisel.

Housing contractor C. G. "Gus" Morrison donated supplies and leftovers from his construction jobs. Leo Gallagher, a Tacoma branch member, bought a huge lot of Army surplus equipment: beds, mattresses, field kits for the kitchen, metal trays, silverware, and the like. The design of the new lodge was modified to take advantage of some large windows donated to the project.

The main lodge construction took place in the summer of 1948. Two large trusses above the main room allowed a clear floor without support posts in the middle. The largest work party—160 people—answered the call for help in putting on the roof; this at a time when the club had 1,600 members. Normal work parties totaled about 30 or 40, and even the children helped haul bricks and other small items.

The winter of 1948–49 was a severe one, with almost twenty feet of snow on the ground at Snoqualmie Pass. But the lodge was so well built that no structural damage could be found the following spring.

The new lodge became a center for not only outdoor sports. Indoors in the evenings, dances were popular. Jack and Catherine Crabill hit upon the idea of what they called bachelor parties. The December 10, 1949, bulletin announced the first affair with this invitation: "All bachelor girls and fellows, present and erstwhile, come to our first party."

Since erstwhile means "former," the party was a huge success, with seventy-six "singles" of all matrimonial persuasions attending. The Crabills also were among the first to bring outside groups to the lodges, which tended to act as a device for recruiting new members.

The dance calendar became almost as important as the other activities the lodge was built for. January featured a New Year's dance party, February a Valentine's party, March a Klondike party, April an April Fool's square dance, and May a lodge festival. Norman Benson, who joined The Mountaineers in 1950 as a young man, said most dances attracted "twice as many gals as guys. . . . For the guys, it was almost too good to be true."

Some of the climbers and skiers weren't getting much sleep with all the dancing going on. A complaint to the board brought action: "The lodge should be made attractive to ALL members. . . . Dancing is not one of the main activities of the club and should never become

the main activity of our lodges." Dances were cut off at ten-thirty or eleven instead of going on until the wee hours.

In the many years since then, the Snoqualmie Lodge has served as a base for winter sports and camaraderie for thousands. Today's lodge is especially welcoming to children, offering a chance for people to socialize in an extended-family atmosphere. Rope tows haul casual skiers up the hill outside, while the serious downhillers head next door to the chairlifts. Friday night is now reserved for organized groups such as Scouts, school and church clubs, women's organizations, and Mountaineers groups. Many of the Friday night participants who are not Mountaineers members later join as a result of their lodge experience.

MEANY SKI HUT

The site chosen for Meany Ski Hut was adjacent to the Northern Pacific Railroad tracks at the eastern end of Stampede Tunnel at the station known as Martin. Edmond Meany bought the land and gave it to the club. His only stipulation: that the hut be closed on Easter Sundays due to the religious observance. That request is still honored.

"The ease with which the hut could be reached, its physical comforts and the fine runs almost at its front door attracted many to whom the rigors of the winter sports had formerly seemed too arduous," Robert Hayes noted in the 1929 annual.

Although at slightly lower elevation than Snoqualmie Pass, Meany Hut is on the eastern slopes of the Cascades where the snow is drier and the skiing better. Outings to Stampede Pass had led some early skiers over the pass and into the Meany area, where the favorable terrain and accessibility by train impressed them. These explorers were enthusiastic over the slopes and magnificent open timber of Meany Hill.

Building materials for the hut were shipped to Martin, unloaded by volunteers, and carried to the site—with some help from the railroad section hands "through the skillful cajolery of W. J. Maxwell plus a small cash consideration." Construction started in September 1928, and on November 11 Meany dedicated the building.

Unlike Snoqualmie Lodge, which was built with much artistic flair, Meany was somewhat spartan. But it served nicely, to judge by a remembrance written by Fred Ball in the 1956 annual: "While rough, it was comfortable, with the big hotel range in the kitchen and the pot-bellied coal stove in the main room giving off a cheery glow; on the wire rack overhead wet socks, mittens and other gear dried or nicely browned, depending on the owner's alertness. Gasoline lanterns furnished light, but after a day of climbing up and sliding down the hills, early to bed was the rule, for tomorrow was another day."

Ball noted that a "mysterious schism among the skiers developed with the advent of the ski hut. Snoqualmie Lodge was a place of gaiety and entertainment as well as skiing, with its huge fireplace, phonograph, and space enough for dancing. Meany Hut, however, was conceived and approved as strictly a shelter for skiers, with no fireplace or extra space. There was plenty of gaiety and fun, but of a different kind, and apparently this difference caused some to prefer one place to the other. Thus, while there were those who alternated, the skiers in general were identified as either 'Lodge hounds' or 'Meanyites.' "

By the winter of 1938–39, a rope tow designed by Jack Hossack had been completed at Meany, with grippers attached to the rope to pull the skier along. The tow was so powerful that many a skier was yanked off his or her feet and dragged up the hill, skis flailing behind

until the person abandoned all hope and let go.

The original conception of Meany Hut as merely a shelter was finally reconsidered. In 1939 a three-story addition provided a basement with a furnace, drying room, waxing room, washroom, and indoor plumbing. The main floor became a recreation room, including space for dancing. The second floor provided separate dormitories for men and women, with married couples quartered on the third floor.

Many of the region's first ski races can be traced back to Meany. Cross-country races for men and women for the University Book Store trophies began in 1929. The first Patrol Race, from Snoqualmie Lodge to Meany Ski Hut, also was run in 1930. Slalom and downhill races for men began that same year, with trophies donated by Bob Hayes and Bill Maxwell. Maxwell, with a nickname of "Wild Bill" earned in part by his skiing technique, competed in the first race for the trophy he sponsored— and came in dead last.

Also achieving legendary status at Meany was Nashie Iverson, wife of a Northern Pacific Railroad engineer. In the early years, it was difficult to find a cook for the weekend outings, but in 1935 the hut committee prevailed upon Nashie to take the job. In 1956, when she wrote a piece for the annual, she still reigned as cook

❧

Right: Nashie Iverson, shown here in 1942, reigned as chief cook and matchmaker at Meany Ski Hut for many years. Much club lore is attributed to Nashie. One example: When a concerned mother called to inquire whether her daughter would be safe in the company of the boys at the hut, Nashie replied, "Oh, they're too tired to do anything anyway." Photo: Mabel Furry, Special Collections, University of Washington Libraries, neg. no. 18150.

and chief matchmaker at the hut.

"I remember the first time I came to Meany," she wrote. "Never in my life had I met such a queer lot of people, was my first impression. Their garb surely set them apart as being out of the ordinary.

"It didn't take long to figure out that outdoor sports were not their only interest; they had an interest in everything! After my day's work, it was interesting for me to sit in the shadows and see the romantic intrigue among the bachelors and spinsters, for there was plenty of it. No one paid much attention to the fact that they were being spied upon. My favorite vantage point was sitting underneath the dripping socks that were hung over the old coal stove. . . ."

A concerned mother once asked Nashie whether her daughter would be safe in the company of the boys at the hut. Nashie assured her that "they're too tired to do anything anyway."

Built at a former railroad camp, Meany Hut was situated to take advantage of the rail line that ran next to it. Train schedules allowed for a full day of skiing, plus time for dinner and cleanup, for members who rode up from Seattle. A special car would be provided for parties of fifteen or more, and that in turn provided all kinds of entertainment on the trip to and from the city.

The coal-burning locomotives were a spectacular sight as they puffed up toward the hut, spewing steam and smoke. The ashes they left behind sometimes littered the slopes, making skiing difficult. And at night, "people would swear the trains ran on both sides of the hut instead of on the tracks," Art Winder recalled, "and some declared they passed through the lower floor."

Rail service was discontinued in 1960, and snow cats have been used since then to tow skiers the two and a half miles from the highway. For more than thirty years the snow-cat driver has been A. T. "Tom" VanDevanter Jr., running what has been dubbed the world's longest ski tow.

Meany Ski Hut continues to operate its rope tows, and runs a busy downhill ski school in January and February. Cross-country sessions and clinics in such techniques as telemarking and snowboarding also are given.

STEVENS SKI LODGE

During World War II many servicemen and women stationed in the Puget Sound area joined The Mountaineers, both to enjoy outdoor recreation and to meet people, and this spurred development of new ski lodges. In May 1946, the board of trustees voted to build facilities at Stevens Pass and Mount Baker in addition to the new Snoqualmie Lodge.

The buildings were intended to be anything but lavish. "All sites will be developed as cheaply as possible, with maximum accommodations for minimum cost," the June 1946 *Mountaineer* bulletin stated.

For Stevens, the site committee selected a sloping lot at 4,200 feet elevation among the group cabin sites made available by Forest Service permit, just west of the Stevens Pass ski area. Under direction of Walter B. Little, construction parties camped out during the summer of 1946 while they worked on the project. Power wouldn't be installed until 1954, so the building was constructed with hand tools. Initially, only cold water was available, piped in from a small creek to the kitchen and washroom.

Stevens Ski Cabin opened in 1948 with thirty-three bunks, and outdoor toilets. The building was only twenty-four feet wide by twenty-six feet long. But it was four stories high, with basement and main floor, plus two stories for dormitories under the steep roof.

In the winter of 1950–51, snow creeping down the slope pushed the cabin into a downhill lean. Guy wires and anchors were installed to remedy the problem—but then winter snows bearing on the cables pulled the cabin in the other direction, so it leaned uphill. Adjustment turnbuckles were then installed to keep the building plumb during periods of heavy snow.

Work parties began an addition in 1953. Power lines reached the building the following year, and the "new" Stevens cabin opened on December 4, 1954. As improvements continued, its designation was upgraded to "lodge."

Stevens Ski Lodge developed its own special atmosphere, to judge by this report in the December 1960 *Bulletin:*

"Skiers arriving after skiing Saturday will find a bowl of popcorn being passed around the stone fireplace. They may also find, upon checking the duty roster, that they will be helping with dinner preparation or serving. During a succulent dinner, classical music from the hut's extensive record collection provides a pleasant atmosphere. After everyone helps clean up the dinner dishes, the records change in mood. Beethoven's symphonies are replaced by schottisches, hambos and polkas. While eager skiers dance off their energy, the more lethargic relax, reading or chatting around the fireplace. In the basement, the ping-pong players hold forth while the wax artists compare notes on the best wax for tomorrow's powder. The early-to-bedders can escape from some of the old-time music by rolling into the third-floor dorms before lights out and all quiet at 11 P.M."

Stevens Ski Lodge now has such amenities as showers and flush toilets and is readily accessible by car. The neighboring commercial ski area, with its eleven chairlifts, offers lodge guests some of the finest downhill skiing in the Cascades.

MOUNT BAKER SKI LODGE

The deepest snow, the longest ski season, magnificent scenery, great downhill and cross-country terrain: In the early 1940s it was obvious that The Mountaineers needed a cabin near the Mount Baker ski runs. Obvious, but not an easy matter. The building sites are at 4,200 feet, and the building season is exceptionally short.

In December 1945 the club rented two cabins above Bagley Lake. To find the cabins in deep snow, each weekend's first arrivals looked for a group of trees with a shovel hanging from one. They used the shovel to dig down to the cabin entrance. These cabins were used until 1949.

The Mountaineers then made arrangements to rent a cabin that was closer to the plowed road. Built in the 1930s as a private summer home, the cabin was on a ridge with a wonderful view of Mount Shuksan and the Canadian border peaks. The wind pattern kept the entrance mostly free of snow, although it also drove snow under the roof shakes, creating little reservoirs that melted and dripped into the cabin.

The cabin was not large enough for the dancing that was so popular at other Mountaineers ski facilities, but reading, knitting, and conversation flourished before the fireplace. Bridge was a favorite pastime when the weather was bad—as it was one New Year's weekend. After two days stuck in the cabin during a storm, Neva Karrick decided to venture outdoors. She returned after an hour or so and was asked how the snow was. "Fine," she said, "quite light."

At that news, skiers scurried to their parkas and ski boots. But the first person to reach the door turned back indignantly, saying, "The wind is blowing so hard the snow is coming down sideways." Neva smiled and said, "You asked *how* the snow was, not where," and went on with her bridge game.

One winter there was an outbreak of petty thievery—unheard of at a Mountaineers facility. Cabin users were missing keys, sunglasses, coins, and watches. The lodge committee went to work examining who used the lodge and when, trying to catch the thief. But they could find no pattern. Finally someone became suspicious of a rustling in the wall and removed some paneling. They discovered a pack-rat nest with all of the missing items carefully stored away.

Meanwhile, Mountaineers were exploring possible sites for a cabin of their own. In April 1956, club president Chester Powell and his successor-to-be, Paul Wiseman, chose a ridge north of the cabin on land that could be leased from the Forest Service.

Architect William Gardner designed a lodge and donated the plans to the club. However, his design came as something of a shock. While virtually all ski lodges in the area were chalet style, with steeply sloping roofs, Gardner's design had a nearly flat roof. Wiseman recalls that Gardner was in a quandary over how to figure the snow stresses on a steep roof, but found it was no problem calculating the stresses on a nearly flat roof. And no matter how much snow was on the roof, it would never tip over. Gardner's design was the one that was chosen.

That September, Don Winslow headed a work party that burned an old barn and cleaned up the site. In June 1958 precut timbers were hauled by logging truck from Seattle up the Mount Baker Highway, the truck crawling along at about ten miles an hour up the grades to the building site. Work party members recall that the truck arrived at 4 A.M., with unloading having to wait until everyone woke up.

Work parties were held each weekend during the summer. The first snowfall coincided with the moving of a gas cookstove into the lodge October 19. The next four work parties installed the picture windows that look out on Mount Shuksan across Picture Lake, completed the basement floor, and finished the tunnel entrance in a snowstorm, with the final work coming just before the Thanksgiving ski weekend. On January 1, 1959, the cabin was formally opened.

Mount Baker Ski Lodge can accommodate sixty-four skiers, who sleep in two upstairs dormitories. There are two bathrooms, a basement drying room with warm air blown in by fan, a workbench for equipment repairs, and storage for skis in the entrance tunnel. Animal-proof storage allows food staples to be brought in during the fall while cars can still get to the lodge.

Lodge users take advantage of the commercial lifts at the adjacent Mount Baker ski area, or go ski touring to such places as Table Mountain, Herman Saddle, and Lake Ann, as well as to Shuksan Arm and other more ambitious destinations. In use year-round, the lodge adapts readily for visits by small parties, families, or larger groups, and makes a convenient base for summer hiking.

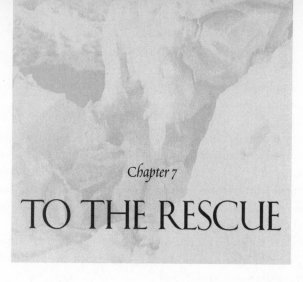

Chapter 7

TO THE RESCUE

When young Delmar Fadden set out on the first winter ascent of Mount Rainier's Emmons Glacier in January 1936, he set off a chain of events that would result in formation of a national mountaineering rescue organization. Although Fadden paid for his daring with his life, his legacy can be appreciated by the thousands of people who have been rescued in the wilderness.

Fadden, an ambitious young climber who had dreamed of climbing Mount Everest, skied into Glacier Basin on the isolated north side of the mountain. When he failed to return, the search that ensued became national news.

Ome Daiber was among those the park rangers called upon to help look for Fadden. In September 1935, a few months before Fadden's ill-fated ascent, Daiber had led the first ascent of Liberty Ridge on Rainier's north face. An outgoing, likable Seattle native, Daiber made friends wherever he went. Newspaper reporters were naturally drawn to him since he was invariably the source of a good quote, and the press quickly focused on him during the search for Fadden.

Fadden's disappearance put the Park Service in a bit of a bind. Though his climb had not been authorized, the rangers were still expected to find him, and they lacked climbers with the expertise to venture out in the middle of winter. Daiber and several others from The Mountaineers responded to their call, with teams leaving from Glacier Basin on one side of the Emmons Glacier and the Summerland meadow on the other. The searchers eventually met at Steamboat Prow, a rock buttress that juts into the Emmons Glacier at about 9,500 feet elevation. It was bitterly cold, and all they could find were the snowshoes Fadden had been carrying and some route-marking wands at about 11,000 feet. At that point, a three-day storm blew in, forcing them to retreat.

After the storm subsided, Fadden's father chartered an airplane so Daiber could continue the search, and from the air he noticed a dark spot on the Emmons Glacier at about 13,000 feet. Closer inspection revealed that it was Fadden's frozen body. He apparently had fallen during the descent, and had probably been knocked unconscious and died of hypothermia.

The body was recovered by a team led by Daiber and ranger Bill Butler that braved sub-zero weather, with most of the members suffering severe frostbite.

In Fadden's pocket was found a roll of exposed film that included pictures of the summit crater, spectacular evidence that he had made it to the top. He is credited with the first winter ascent of the Emmons. (Fadden's namesake nephew later became president of The Mountaineers; that Delmar Fadden served as president for two years in the mid-1980s.)

Daiber himself gained firsthand experience of the need for rescue on the Fadden trip when a huge boulder rolled over his left foot on the hike in to the mountain. Though he continued the climb, the injury would plague him for the rest of his life. Daiber seldom mentioned it, and many of his future climbing partners were not even aware of the debilitating injury.

Following this heroic and heavily publicized rescue effort, Daiber and an informal group of his climbing friends continued to make mountain rescues until 1939, when The Mountaineers formed the Mountaineer Rescue Patrol. The club's stated policy was that the patrol would be mobilized only for cases requiring technical climbing skills. Members of The Mountaineers were provided a list of rescue volunteers they could call for help. Cases involving non-members would be handled only if requested by an appropriate agency.

Rescuers who were called out, sometimes in the middle of the night, gathered at the clubrooms as soon as possible, the injured person's family was notified and, if necessary, the Highway Patrol was asked to provide a speedy escort to the trailhead. In most cases, a second group would start soon after the first, to establish a camp, take in food, make a trail, and support the initial rescuers.

The leader of the rescue patrol, appointed at the clubrooms, would have complete authority at all times and his decisions would not be questioned unless for obvious reasons. The injured person was brought down to a trail, where Forest Service rangers or Civilian Conservation

Corps workers would get the person to a waiting ambulance.

Daiber remained the front man for these rescues. His charismatic personality made him the perfect spokesman, and he was hard to refuse when he called on someone to leave their job or jump out of bed and dash down to the clubrooms. After 1940, when he married Matie Johnson, whom he had met on the 1939 summer outing to the Grand Tetons, the group often operated from the Daibers' kitchen table. There

Larry Penberthy, Matie and Ome Daiber (in front), Bernie Pearson,* and Joe Firey pose for a picture at Spray Park on Mount Rainier in 1979. Penberthy used his engineering skills to produce innovative gear for climbers. The Daibers and other club members ran a club-sponsored mountain rescue service from their kitchen table until it became formally organized as the Mountain Rescue Council. Ome Daiber, who invented SnowSeal boot sealant, made the first ascent of Mount Rainier's Liberty Ridge in 1934. Joe Firey is well known for first ascents, especially on skis. Photo: Dee Molenaar, Joe Firey collection.

Matie would get on the phone and organize impromptu rescue missions at any hour of the day or night. To alert rescue-team members, she recruited a phone committee of former women climbers who had been "grounded" by family responsibilities (referred to as the "call girls" until some members protested).

For their efforts, these volunteers got paid absolutely nothing, and furthermore were expected to provide the rescue equipment, some of which was costly. In a 1982 interview, Daiber proclaimed, "I've never charged a dime, and I never would. We pay our own way."

After World War II, Wolf Bauer, the early skier who had helped start the climbing course, visited his native Bavaria, where he saw a film on Innsbruck's Bergwacht, the crack mountain guards on the German–Austrian border. He was so taken with it that he brought a copy back home. Along with Otto Trott of the Ski Patrol, who had also come to the Northwest from the European Alps, he called Daiber's group together to watch the film.

The rescue members didn't need to understand German to be awed by the climbing and rescue techniques shown in the film, which illustrated just how dated the methods being used in the Pacific Northwest were. They set out to learn and employ improved rescue methods. Soon afterward, the group formed the nation's first Mountain Rescue Council, using Mountaineer Rescue Patrol volunteers as a nucleus. These included Bauer, Trott, Arne Campbell, Max Eckenburg, Dorrell Looff, Kurt Beam, and Jack Hossack, among others. The council was officially formed in the spring of 1948 under sponsorship of The Mountaineers, the Washington Alpine Club, and the Northwest region of the National Ski Patrol.

The Mountaineers soon became aware of the need for establishing closer contact with government agencies to coordinate rescue efforts. The club sent personal letters to all National Park Service and Forest Service supervisors and district rangers in the Northwest—more than sixty in all—to explain their desire to stay in touch. Copies of the "Climber's Notebook" and the *Mountaineer* annual were enclosed, and the

Ome Daiber, Dr. Otto Trott, and Wolf Bauer, shown in about 1950, were the founders of the Seattle Mountain Rescue and Safety Council, later renamed the Mountain Rescue Council. Composed of expert skiers and experienced mountain climbers, this voluntary group served as a model for the national organization. Trott, a surgeon, who also founded the Mount Baker Ski Patrol in 1939 and made a first ascent of Shuksan's Hanging Glacier, had a notable climbing career in the Dolomites and Tyrolean Alps of Europe before immigrating to the United States in 1937. Trott and Bauer both used their skills and European contacts to spark major advances in climbing and skiing in the Northwest.
Photo: Ira Spring.

Members of the Mountain Rescue and Safety Council and a U.S. Coast Guard helicopter crew conduct a practice rescue in 1949. They include Chuck Welsh (standing far left), Dee Molenaar (next to him), Cornelius "K" Molenaar* (fourth from left), Ome Daiber (center with beret), Jim Whittaker (right), and Lou Whittaker (kneeling third from left). Photo: Dee Molenaar collection.

officials were put on the mailing list of the *Mountaineer* bulletin, which included a monthly listing of all club climbs and activities.

In June 1948, the first of several Northwest Mountaineering Conferences was called to explore ways to coordinate the rescue efforts of local, state, federal, and military agencies. The first two-day conference was well attended by all major mountaineering clubs in Washington, Oregon, and British Columbia. All eight of the government agencies invited also turned out in force. The conferences were the impetus for a great deal of innovative work.

Pioneering work was done in developing communications, with Motorola FM Handie-Talkie sets modified to enable air-ground messages to be sent between the rescue units and the rescue base. Various types of stretchers were tested, but most of them were found wanting. The boat-type stretcher used by the Ski Patrol worked well on snow but was nearly useless on a rocky trail. Therefore, Wolf Bauer and Jack Hossack went to work on a new design, with the help of Wally Burr, a ski maker whose family had long belonged to the club. What emerged from Burr's basement workshop was a collapsible stretcher that could be broken down and carried by two rescuers and that could operate with either a ski or a wheel at the bottom.

Missions were expanded beyond club members to anyone needing rescue in difficult mountain environments, with lowland rescues being left

Wallace "Wally" Burr skis near Snoqualmie Lodge
in the early 1920s. Burr, a master craftsman,
introduced the banana water ski in the early 1950s.
He is credited with starting the water-skiing
revolution and catapulting the Puget Sound water-ski
industry to world dominance (the founders of the
O'Brien and Connelly ski companies were
his protégés). Burr, with help from Wolf Bauer and
Jack Hossack, also designed the Stokeski stretcher
of Mountain Rescue fame. Photo: Album,
The Mountaineers Archives.

to other organizations. While rescues weren't very frequent in the first few years of the Mountain Rescue Council's existence, in 1952 and 1953 the group began to feel the brunt of the rapidly increasing recreational use of the wilderness. During those two years, more than fifteen full-scale rescues were mounted for accidents due to avalanches, lightning strikes, crevasse falls, glissades, cliff falls, rappelling mishaps, and rockfall—plus four airplane crashes, which claimed forty lives.

After that, branch units of the Mountain Rescue Council were enrolled on both sides of the Cascades—in the Washington towns of Bellingham, Bremerton, Everett, Longview, Tacoma, and Yakima, and in Portland, Oregon. More than forty new rescue members were recruited and trained. In addition, members went forth with an almost missionary zeal to help recruit rescue teams in other regions.

In 1959, the national Mountain Rescue Association was formed, with teams spreading out over Alaska, Idaho, Montana, Colorado, Arizona, California, and New Mexico.

The Mountain Rescue Council's largest-scale rescue came the following year, in 1960, when Pete Schoening and brothers Lou and Jim Whittaker were involved in a fall near the summit of Alaska's Mount McKinley, along with John Day, whom they were guiding on a one-day speed climb of McKinley. The group was descending the West Buttress after successfully reaching the summit when Jim Whittaker slipped, pulling the others off their feet. John Day suffered a broken leg in the fall, and Schoening was knocked unconscious and later lost several of his fingertips to frostbite.

Another team of climbers was nearby and reported the accident. Fifty-four climbers representing the Mountain Rescue Councils in Washington and Oregon ended up flying to

Ed Boulton (foreground) practices rescue techniques at a Mountain Rescue Council seminar on Mount Erie in Anacortes. Photo: Stella Degenhardt.

Alaska in response to the emergency involving some of the Northwest's best-known mountaineers. Schoening and Day, the most seriously injured, were evacuated by helicopter from 17,200 feet, a feat that had never been accomplished before, and the Whittakers were helped down to safety.

However, a severe storm blew in, trapping twenty of the rescuers for ten days and pointing up the need for special radios and frequencies specifically for rescue use. Hundreds of such radios are now on the air throughout the national Mountain Rescue Association system.

Among other notable operations involving the Mountain Rescue Council was the evacuation of a badly injured climber, Peter Potterfield, from a tiny ledge on the face of the North Cascades' Chimney Rock in July 1988. Potterfield, his left shoulder and arm shattered after a nearly rope-length leader fall, tied himself to the ledge while his partner went for help.

The rescue ultimately took the help of twenty-five climbers and rescue professionals from four cities, ham radio operators, the Red Cross, the Forest Service, two military bases, and the Kittitas County sheriff. Once aid reached Potterfield, it required more than six hours to lower him to the Chimney Glacier, where rescuers literally threw his litter into a military helicopter that could only hover on the steep snow. The rescue succeeded thanks to an emergency response system put in place through efforts of the Mountain Rescue Council.

The Council and The Mountaineers cooperated in publishing an English-language edition of Wastl Mariner's *Mountain Rescue Techniques* in 1964, with translation by Otto Trott and Kurt Beam and editing by Harvey Manning. The book was reprinted in Austria with the cooperation of the Austrian Alpine Club, and the translation and updating were so good that the International Commission for Alpine Rescue adopted the text for use worldwide.

The Mountaineers continues to support Seattle Mountain Rescue with a representative on its board and annual donations.

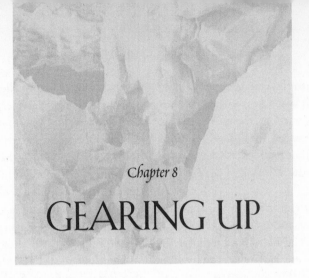

Chapter 8

GEARING UP

On Edmond Meany's last club climb, an overnighter to Mount Ellinor in the Olympics in 1929, the climber who happened to pitch his tent next to Meany's was a new member on only his second climb with The Mountaineers, Lloyd Anderson. During that chance encounter, the past and future of Northwest mountaineering rubbed shoulders.

Anderson was among those who a few years later would help overthrow the old guard and catapult The Mountaineers into the forefront of American mountaineering. He was among the first to climb all six of the state's major peaks in a single season, thereby upsetting the club's established way of doing things. And along with his wife, Mary, he would structure the climbing course along the basic lines that it retains sixty years later. But Lloyd and Mary Anderson had one other achievement for which they are likely to be much better remembered: They founded Recreational Equipment Inc.

REI's 1998 membership soars into the millions, and the cooperative has stores from coast to coast, expanding far beyond its beginnings and original purposes. The Andersons' fundamental reason for forming the cooperative was to get quality equipment into the hands of climbers as cheaply as possible. In that they

succeeded as perhaps no one else has.

Lloyd Anderson graduated from the University of Washington in 1926 with a degree in electrical engineering, only to find that jobs in his chosen profession had evaporated during his student years. In 1928, he finally landed a job with Seattle Transit, where he would remain for thirty-two years, but with little professional reward. He was chronically bored by the time he joined the club in 1929. The climbing course would rescue him from that boredom. Both he and Mary enrolled in the first course in 1935.

All of Lloyd's previous climbing, including Mount Rainier, had been done with an alpenstock. But the type of climbing being taught by Wolf Bauer was more technical, and an ice ax had great advantages over an alpenstock. The problem was, ice axes were expensive and the selection was limited.

"We had a few dinky little stores that sold stuff," Lloyd said in 1996 of the outdoor recreation selection available in 1935. But they didn't sell much, and what they did sell was at exorbitant cost. He found an Austrian-made ice ax at the OutDoor Store, the traditional Mountaineers supply outlet, but he found the twenty-dollar price tag outrageous.

Lloyd kept hunting and was told at another

Lloyd and Mary Anderson model the very latest in mountainwear for a 1946 newspaper photo. The caption reads: "The Smart Set." Lloyd was club president at the time, and the cooperative they founded in 1938 (later known as Recreational Equipment Inc.) was one of the best sources of mountaineering gear in the country. The Anderson family devoted years to making the cooperative a thriving concern. Today, REI is a nationwide chain and still functions as a cooperative, refunding a portion of its profits to members each year. In the late 1930s, Lloyd and Mary (who served long stints on the club's board) established the basic structure of the climbing course—a structure it retains today. Photo: Seattle Post-Intelligencer.

small shop, Cunningham's, that he could get an Austrian-made ice ax for seven dollars. Even that was a good deal of money in the days when many workers earned fifty cents an hour, but he relented and ordered the ice ax. However, when he went in to pick it up just before the climbing course began, what was handed to him was not an Austrian-made work of art but a Japanese knockoff, and the price had gone up to twelve dollars.

Lloyd couldn't help but feel he'd been slickered, and his prominent jaw turned rock hard as he dug deep into his wallet. It was either that or go without, and he had already determined that the testing grounds of human character were on mountain rock and snow. Lloyd kept grumbling about the incident until a fellow climber, Swiss-born Rudy Amsler, informed him of European magazines that carried ads for climbing equipment the way Pacific Northwest magazines carried ads for hunting rifles. A catalog from Sporthaus Peterlongo in Innsbruck, Austria, was soon delivered to the Andersons' front door.

Mary knew enough German to be able to translate the equipment descriptions and convert schillings to dollars. But to Lloyd, with his crummy twelve-dollar ice ax, her translation seemed all wrong. Mary insisted she was right, and so they sent off for the genuine Austrian ice ax Lloyd longed for. When it arrived, delivered to their doorstep by the postman, it turned out to be a superb example of European mountaineering technology. The cost: three dollars and fifty cents, postage-paid.

Lloyd's jaw set up rock hard once again as he realized just how much money the middlemen were making with their monopoly on mountain gear.

Fellow climbers who saw Lloyd's new ice ax quite naturally wanted one of their own, and it wasn't long before a visit to the Anderson home meant you were liable to be seated on a crate, bearing a European postmark, that had arrived filled with ice axes, crampons, pitons, and carabiners. Lloyd and Mary's living room business was launched. Lloyd didn't see himself in competition with established outdoor stores. In fact, he didn't see himself in business at all. It was a pastime for him, something to take his mind off his job. He would import the gear for himself and his friends, charge precisely what he had paid plus a tiny cushion to cover unforeseen costs, and turn the goods over with a handshake.

But this could not go on forever since Lloyd had too many friends and was making more fast as word spread. The venture had to be formalized. So with the help of Seattle attorney Ed Rombauer, who believed in the Depression-era cooperative movement to the extent that he charged no fees for helping people set up cooperatives, Lloyd hatched his plan.

On June 23, 1938, five Mountaineers met at Rombauer's office, and each paid one dollar to join Recreational Equipment Cooperative. Lloyd and Mary were issued cards No. 1 and 2; Rombauer himself joined, taking card No. 3; No. 4 went to Walt Hoffman; No. 5 went to Ed Kennedy; No. 6 to Helen Rudy. The idea was that the members themselves would be the owners, receiving a dividend each year according to what they had spent at the co-op, rather than according to how much stock they had purchased in the company.

During the first year, Recreational Equipment was nothing more than a shelf at the Puget Sound Cooperative Store, a farmers' co-op situated just north of the Pike Place Market in Seattle. Brotherhood was the word of the day, and the Cooperative Store at first took no fee for selling the recreation equipment for free.

But as volume grew, Lloyd granted the store a 5 percent commission.

When the idealistic Puget Sound Cooperative Store failed, Recreational Equipment moved to Julius Ruen's gas station on Western Avenue just behind the Market. It was another brotherhood venture. Members could save 2 cents per gallon on gasoline by going to the station and saying they belonged to the co-op. And while they were getting gas, they could wander in and gawk at the mountain goods. It was an honor system; you took what you wanted off the shelf and wrote your own receipt. Incredibly, the system worked.

In 1942, when the gas station was sold and the new owners demanded a higher commission, Lloyd balked. Instead, he found space just down the hall from The Mountaineers clubrooms above the Green Apple Pie Cafe at 523½ Pike Street. There, another dollar-

In 1942 the club moved to 523½ Pike Street, just above the Green Apple Pie Cafe. Soon thereafter, Lloyd Anderson moved his fledgling Recreational Equipment Cooperative down the hall, thereby establishing a kind of Mountaineers Central. The club and the co-op soon became identified as one, with the co-op commonly referred to as "The Mountaineers Co-op," even though there was no direct relationship between the club and the co-op. Photo: REI collection.

conscious tenant, accountant Adam Mayer, was willing to share his space for the established 5 percent commission.

During World War II, the Andersons managed to maintain a full equipment list in part by manufacturing some of the gear themselves. From the family kitchen came a popular fire starter, Kindlestix, along with plastic bags of dehydrated vegetables. Lloyd's basement workshop produced ice-ax handles, with the heads forged by a local blacksmith. On her home sewing machine, Mary turned out tents patterned after the Appalachian Mountain Tent, called the Co-op Mountain Tent. Lloyd erected the tents using collapsible poles made from aluminum tubing.

The outdoor recreation boom that followed World War II turned the co-op into a flourishing enterprise. When Lloyd began the cooperative in 1938, Mountaineers membership was about 500 members. Ten years later, the club roster was up to 2,263. In 1949, membership in the co-op—now at 2,688—outpaced that of the club that had spawned it. Co-op sales in 1945 totaled $8,797, in 1946 $23,714, and in 1949 $31,354.

In 1956, Recreational Equipment Cooperative was incorporated, acknowledging the fact that it had turned into a serious business and needed to provide litigation protection for those associated with it. State law prevented use of the word Cooperative in the name, so it became Recreational Equipment Inc., or the familiar REI.

Dick McGowan had been hired in 1954 as the first manager of the co-op store. But the next spring when Norman Dyrenfurth passed through town recruiting climbers for a Himalayan expedition, McGowan couldn't resist the lure of Lhotse and left the job. His successor was Jim Whittaker. Jim and his identical twin brother Lou had joined The Mountaineers in 1944 through the Boy Scouts and participated in mountain rescues while still attending West Seattle High School. In fact, Lloyd had taken the Whittaker twins on their first climb, of the Tooth near Snoqualmie Pass, when they were fifteen years old.

On July 25, 1955, Jim Whittaker took McGowan's old job at REI. The pay was four hundred dollars a month, the work week a full seven days. Whittaker's friends tried to talk him out of it, telling him that a guy with his charisma and talent could write his own ticket. What they didn't factor in was Lloyd's dictum that his top employee would be expected to keep up with his climbing and skiing. What other boss would have insisted that Whittaker spend time in the mountains? So he began twenty-four years with REI.

In 1963, when Whittaker climbed Mount Everest, the national exposure that came with being the first American to stand atop the world's highest mountain offered REI so much free advertising that the following year, 1964, its gross income topped $1 million for the first time. The REI board in the 1950s included a distinguished group of current and past leaders of The Mountaineers. Seven of them had served as climbing chairmen, and only one was not a widely known club figure. The board didn't have much to do, as Lloyd made all the decisions, so they just cheered him on.

Lloyd had envisioned REI as the purest form of democracy, the membership assembling periodically to discuss the co-op's future and make decisions. It didn't quite work out that way. Instead, it became difficult to get a legal quorum at the annual meetings, in spite of bribes such as free food, door prizes, and color

The Whittaker twins, Jim and Lou, shown with chief Rainier guide Bill Dunaway (left) in 1951, joined The Mountaineers as Boy Scouts and received much of their early mountaineering training through the club's climbing course. Jim became head of REI and in 1963 was the first American to reach the summit of Mount Everest. Lou owns and runs the guide service on Mount Rainier. Photo: Ira Spring.

slides of Mountaineers outings. The members were quite content to leave all the work to Lloyd, Mary, and Jim.

However, things began to change after 1964 and the first million-dollar year. Board meetings that had been storytelling sessions, with the actual work decided in a few minutes, took on the aspect of corporate meetings. But there had never been quite such an enterprise as REI, and the directors were uncertain how to manage it. The sixteenfold growth in the ten years that followed Whittaker's ascent of Everest wouldn't

make things easier. Under Whittaker's leadership, REI's role as a national company increased, with outlets opening in other parts of the country. REI slowly accepted professional business guidance and its current leadership revolves around personnel recruited from the business world rather than the mountaineering fraternity.

However, the original premise of the co-op remains intact. It still refunds about 10 percent of its members' annual purchases each year in the form of dividends.

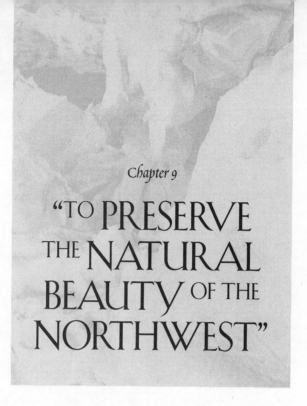

Chapter 9

"TO PRESERVE THE NATURAL BEAUTY OF THE NORTHWEST"

By the time The Mountaineers was formed in 1906, an astonishing amount of the Pacific Northwest's old-growth forest had already been cut. Trees were logged just as fast as roads and sluiceways could be built, and loggers were headed ever deeper into the mountains. The devastation was remarkable, with trees routinely cut off twelve or fifteen feet above the ground because it was faster for loggers to saw through the trunks at that height. The carnage was little publicized, and it wasn't until autos came into wide use that the public was able to visit the logging sites and see the environmental disaster for themselves.

In 1906, the situation was rapidly worsening. The recent development of high-lead logging began to threaten any hopes preservationists had of saving the vast tracts of native forest. Under this system, the top of a spar tree was trimmed high above the ground, then pulleys and cables were attached to it so the logs could be raised up and hauled clear of stumps and debris to a landing. This not only greatly speeded up logging, since the trees didn't have to be skidded out, but it allowed trees to be profitably logged on steep slopes that horses couldn't reach.

By 1910, high-lead logging was in full swing and Washington had become the nation's number one lumber-producing state. The forest products industry accounted for 63 percent of the state's wage jobs, so public sentiment for doing anything about these practices was virtually nonexistent. To many Pacific Northwesterners of the time, tree stumps symbolized prosperity. Builders hacked out town sites from the forest and left the burned out stumps to smolder in the middle of newly graded streets. The timber, mining, and railroad industries heavily promoted such practices as the best use of the land, arguing

⚮

Above: On the summit of Mount St. Helens during the 1922 outing, having completed their ascent of Washington's six major peaks: Leo Gallagher, Margaret Hargrave, Howard Fuller, and William B. Remey. Gallagher, a Tacoma branch member who bought and donated property for the Tacoma clubhouse in the early 1950s, was a pioneer in nearly every major conservation effort of his time. In the 1930s he was a main force behind establishing the influential Federation of Western Outdoor Clubs; in 1948 he was one of the founders of Olympic Park Associates; and in 1968 he was one of seven incorporators of The Mountaineers Foundation. His financial backing of the first edition of Mountaineering: The Freedom of the Hills *was crucial to the ultimate success of Mountaineers Books. Photo: Mabel Furry, Special Collections, University of Washington Libraries, neg. no. 18130.*

⚮

Left: Edward Sturgis Ingraham, shown here in 1922, was a charter member of The Mountaineers. By the time of the club's formation, he was already a well-known mountaineer, having climbed Mount Rainier several times. He is responsible for many of the place names in Mount Rainier National Park, including Summerland, Elysian Fields, and Camp Muir, where in 1888 he camped with John Muir. Ingraham Glacier is named after him. In 1911, Ingraham organized the first Boy Scout troop in the Northwest and led his Scouts on numerous mountain trips, though by that time he was in his sixties. Photo: Mabel V. Nash, Special Collections, University of Washington Libraries, neg. no. 18148.

that wilderness areas were uninhabitable anyway, and so their only value was for the resources that could be extracted from them. The idea that an individual or business had any responsibility to future generations was unknown.

Unknown, that is, except among a few groups, including The Mountaineers. Most of the founding members shared an intensity of purpose that nature's gems must be preserved. The club's first president, Henry Landes, issued the call for the conservation battles that would follow when he wrote in the 1907–08 annual that the organization hoped "to render a public service in the battle to preserve our natural scenery from wanton destruction."

The Mountaineers laid out the club's conservation objectives in its constitution: "To preserve by the encouragement of protective legislation and otherwise the natural beauty of the Northwest coast of America."

The club shared this philosophy with a growing national movement. Nature-loving Theodore Roosevelt, U.S. president at the time of the club's founding, responded to the terrible waste of the nineteenth-century's westward expansion by making conservation one of his top priorities. On the Pacific Coast, the San Francisco–based Sierra Club, the Mazamas in Portland, and The Mountaineers responded to this call and introduced the idea of wilderness preservation.

The Sierra Club came first, formed in 1892 by a small group of professors and other professionals from the San Francisco area who were interested in both climbing and conservation. The Sierra Club was the first in the nation to widely publicize the fact that the natural beauty and resources of the Pacific Coast mountains were being blasted, burned, and used up at an incredible rate.

The Mazamas, on the other hand, tended to put mountaineering first. The club was founded in 1894 when a group of 163 convened on the summit of Mount Hood. All of them thereby met the main requirement for membership, which was proof that you had climbed a glaciated peak. Climbing would remain the club's most important mission, in keeping with its name, which is derived from an early native word for mountain goat. However, the Mazamas would go on to make some important environmental contributions, such as fighting a plan to build a tramway to the top of Mount Hood.

Like the other two clubs, The Mountaineers tried to balance its stake in conservation with its desire for greater accessibility to the mountains. This paradox was recognized from the start. While Landes wanted the club to oppose wanton destruction, he also sought to make wilderness areas "accessible to the largest number of mountain lovers."

All three clubs working together succeeded in promoting the recreational opportunities and the scenic value of the mountains, which would prove to be a lasting contribution. Together, the clubs' annual outings drew thousands of people into the wilderness, and the publicity that resulted did a great deal to sway public perception in favor of recreation and away from commercial exploitation. The outings allowed the budding conservation movement to gain wider acceptance and set the stage for the titanic battles over resources that would follow.

The Mountaineers was quick to support the Sierra Club in its futile effort to prevent the construction of Hetch Hetchy Dam in California's Yosemite National Park. It was a somewhat frivolous project designed to bring water and power to San Francisco, but a less pristine mountain valley would have served the same purpose. Letters were also written concerning the establishment of Glacier National Park in Montana, and assistance was given to writer and naturalist Enos Mills in his attempt to establish Rocky Mountain National Park. In 1912, at the request of the secretary of the interior, The Mountaineers sent a representative to a meeting of national park superintendents at Yosemite and argued forcefully against schemes to turn the national parks into urban-style playgrounds with sideshows that included jazz bands and bear fights. In 1914, the club formed its own legislative committee to deal specifically with preservation issues in the national and state legislatures.

As conservation pioneers, the Mountaineers had a seminal influence on related organizations. Shortly after the club was formed, members established a committee to organize a Northwest chapter of the Audubon Society. With the assistance of the club, in 1911 charter member E. S. Ingraham organized the Boy Scouts of America for the region. The club's Leo Gallagher, a Tacoma branch member, was a main force in the 1930s behind establishing the influential Federation of Western Outdoor Clubs, an alliance of outdoor groups on the Pacific Coast.

Stephen Mather, the first director of the National Park Service, admired the tenacity of The Mountaineers. After warning club members in the 1919 annual of the dangers posed by timber cutting in the Pacific Northwest, Mather gave this encouragement: "Go to it, Mountaineers! There is still time."

His comments were polite window dressing, however, since Mather was the nation's foremost proponent of development in national parks. He didn't see them as areas worthy of preservation so much as resorts where urbanites could get away for entertainment and distraction.

His policies of granting monopoly concessions in the parks would eventually be successfully challenged by The Mountaineers.

OLYMPIC NATIONAL PARK

One of the earliest and longest-lasting of the club's environmental battles was over creation of a national park in the Olympics, which The Mountaineers ironically helped open to exploration with the first summer outing. The subsequent publicity alerted industrial concerns to the relative ease of access, which before that time had been considered extremely difficult.

What initially drew public attention to the Olympics was the indiscriminate slaughter of the once vast Olympic elk herds, and this became a rallying cry for the preservationists. In 1904, U.S. Rep. Francis Cushman of Tacoma introduced a bill for an Elk National Park, but it was blocked because of provisions that would have prevented logging. Later proposals, though without provisions to protect timber that was vital as habitat for the elk, also failed.

Carsten Lien, in his book *Olympic Battleground*, describes early Mountaineers' efforts to stop destruction of the Olympic forests: In February 1909, "Wealthy and influential Seattle attorney George E. Wright, on behalf of a committee of The Mountaineers, undertook to get a national park established on the Olympic Peninsula. . . . Wright wrote to [U.S. Rep. William E.] Humphrey with the authority of God: 'I am about to lend my support to the movement to create some kind of a National Park out of the main body of the Olympic Mountains.' "

Humphrey, who had previously introduced what Lien describes as "save-the-wildlife-but-keep-their habitat-available-for-the-timber-industry legislation," read the message that a park was coming and enlisted in the ranks of the preservationists. He introduced a bill in the House of Representatives to create the park. President Theodore Roosevelt favored the bill, but Congress, heavily indebted to industrial interests, refused to back it.

With Wright's encouragement, Humphrey went to Roosevelt two days before the president's term in office was to expire. Humphrey suggested Roosevelt use his authority under the Antiquities Act to establish a national monument in the Olympics, despite the fact that such monuments

∞

Canvas tents and wool clothing were the stuff of early outings, not exactly light going. Horses were used to pack the gear to base camp. Shown on the 1913 outing to the Olympics: J. Harry Weer, Irving Clark, and Leland Clark. Weer was one of the founders of the Tacoma branch. Irving Clark, a longtime trustee of the club, was an early environmental leader and went on to become one of the founders of The Wilderness Society. Photo: Irving Clark, Special Collections, University of Washington Libraries, neg. no. 18117.

had before that been established only for places of historical interest.

In the 1909 *Mountaineer* annual, Humphrey recalled Roosevelt as saying to him: "Tell me what you want, Mr. Humphrey, and I will give it to you. Do not take time to give me the details, simply tell me what you wish to do."

"Mr. President," Humphrey replied, "I want you to set aside as a national monument 750,000 acres in the heart of the Olympic mountains; the main purpose of this is to preserve the elk of the Olympics."

Roosevelt replied, "I will do it! Prepare your order and I will sign it." This was done.

However, the proposed monument met with overwhelming opposition. Mining and timber interests sought congressional action to abolish the entire dedicated area, attacking The Mountaineers and its allies as radicals and "mushy aesthetes," a derogatory reference to the academics in their ranks.

Wright conferred with fellow club members Edward Allen and Irving Clark and sought a political compromise to salvage what they could of the Olympic preserve. He wrote to the secretary of the interior asking him to establish a blue-ribbon committee involving the special interests and The Mountaineers. However, these negotiations were doomed from the start; Forest Service chief Gifford Pinchot structured the proclamation so it would allow logging and mining.

Mountaineers founding member Asahel Curtis ran into problems with the club when he tried to get members to support the reduced boundaries for the proposed park. Not only did the club reject his recommendations outright, but his efforts also cost him the confidence of the membership and he failed in his bid to gain reelection to the board of trustees. The timber-dominated Seattle Chamber of Commerce

Charter member George E. Wright stands before a Douglas-fir with a nine-foot-diameter trunk along the Elwha trail during the 1913 outing to Mount Olympus. Wright, a prominent Seattle attorney, fought to get a national park established in the Olympics. Photo: Charles Albertson, Special Collections, University of Washington Libraries, neg. no. 18158.

opposed any kind of designation that would protect the Olympic Peninsula, and was not above devious means to achieve its ends. To Curtis, a stalwart Chamber of Commerce supporter, was given the task of persuading the preservationists to give up their fight and to accept the park compromise.

"I can assure you," he told The Mountaineers, "that the park set aside as requested will be a very beautiful one and we are not giving up anything that would be of material benefit to it." What he failed to mention was that logging, placer mining, and road building were contemplated for it.

The Chamber issued a report in January 1912 that openly proposed allowing mining, cutting of timber, the use of water power, and the "right to build and operate any class of transportation . . . through or out of the proposed park," meaning roads and railroads. The elk that started the whole battle had long since been forgotten as the political factions got down to the economic imperatives.

On May 11, 1915, President Wilson signed a proclamation reducing by half the monument as originally proposed, and excluding all of its merchantable timber. Because of this, Curtis was more or less ostracized from the club. Curtis had already commented earlier to naturalist Enos Mills regarding "a number of the members who have taken a strong dislike to me."

Strong dislike was probably putting it mildly. From that point on, Curtis and The Mountaineers would adamantly oppose each other on virtually every major environmental issue that would come up over the next thirty years and more. Curtis himself would go on to become president of Washington Good Roads, and in the 1920s and 1930s he fought vigorously against expansion of the proposed Olympic National Park, as well as opposing the creation of

a national park in the North Cascades. Much of Curtis's work as a photographer came from timber, mining, road building, and agricultural concerns, and that was where his sympathies were. He simply was not a preservationist.

As an example, he felt that a long-term plan to improve Mount Rainier National Park's infrastructure was the most urgent issue of the Washington mountains, a notion scoffed at by other club members. His scheme included resort hotels on the northern slopes and a highway encircling the mountain. The Mountaineers turned against these proposals after the betrayals involving Mount Olympus National Monument, and neither idea ever came about, in large part because of the club's opposition.

The national monument was created, but the fight was far from over. It wasn't long before shock waves passed through the Seattle business community when former Seattle mayor Richard Ballinger, who had been appointed U.S. Secretary of the Interior, unexpectedly took the position that because the monument had been established under the Antiquities Act, no mining or logging could be allowed. This rigid preservationist view about the meaning of the act, which was upheld by his successor, effectively nullified the subterfuge that Curtis and the Chamber of Commerce had crafted—only to be subverted by the Forest Service, which included all of the monument's trees in its logging plan.

Ironically, when Olympic National Park was finally established in 1938, it included an increase in size over the monument almost equal to what had been lost earlier. By that time, the club's active participation in environmental issues was waning during a period of slumping membership caused by the Depression, and it had little say in the creation of the park. Powerful East Coast preservation groups that

Edward W. Allen, walking on the beach around 1912, joined the club in 1910 and was vice president for thirteen years. He was made an honorary member of the club in 1961. In 1920, along with Seattle Mayor Robert Moran, he pushed a bill through the state legislature establishing Moran State Park. An attorney, Allen was also instrumental in efforts leading to establishment of Olympic National Park and formulated the provisions in the late 1920s that were adopted by the National Park Service for preservation of wilderness areas in Mount Rainier National Park. Photo: Thomas Allen collection.

∞

John Osseward, Grant Conway, Sigurd Olsen,* Polly Dyer, and Paul Wiseman on the "William O.
Douglas Hike" in 1958. Supreme Court Justice Douglas led a party of seventy-two prominent
environmental leaders and hikers on a three-day walk along the Olympic wilderness beaches from
Cape Alava to Rialto Beach. His aim was to gain publicity for protecting one of the
last remaining roadless areas of Pacific Coast beach.*

*Dyer, the chief organizer of the walk, has been one of the most prominent and influential environmentalists
in the state of Washington for more than forty years. In addition to becoming chair of The Mountaineers
Conservation Committee in the late 1950s, she served as president of Olympic Park Associates for
twenty-one years, was the first non-Californian on the national Sierra Club board, helped found the North
Cascades Conservation Council, and was a key activist in the effort to create the Alpine Lakes Wilderness
in the 1970s and pass the Washington Wilderness Act in 1984.*

*Osseward, awarded an honorary membership in 1954, began testifying before congressional committees
beginning in the 1930s about the need for wilderness and parks in the Northwest and for keeping national
forest timber cuts within sustainable levels. He helped found Olympic Park Associates in 1948, was a
founding member of The Mountaineers Foundation, a board member of the Wilderness Society and the
National Parks and Conservation Association, and was made an honorary member of the Sierra Club.*

Photo: Olas Murie, The Mountaineers Archives.

Philip Zalesky was an early member of The Mountaineers Conservation Committee, beginning in 1954, and has played a major role in many key Northwest conservation efforts. He was one of the founders of the North Cascades Conservation Council and served as its first president, was president of Olympic Park Associates, and has been active with The Mountaineers Foundation. Photo: Philip Zalesky collection.

had the ear of President Franklin D. Roosevelt were the ones who gathered the support for an 898,000-acre national park over the strident objections of local special interest groups, who wanted no park at all.

The Mountaineers later got back in action and played a pivotal role in securing the long-term protection of Olympic National Park. Unknown to the public, the National Park Service had opposed creation of the park at the same time that FDR and Secretary of the Interior Harold Ickes had been pressing for it. In 1952, the Park Service director authorized the park superintendent to undertake "salvage" logging within its boundaries. The result was the stripping in the mid-1950s of more than 100 million board feet of lumber from the park.

The Mountaineers did not discover what was happening until Paul Shepard, executive secretary of the Garden Clubs of America, became

head seasonal ranger at the park in the summer of 1956 and witnessed the damage being done. Shepard overcame the reluctance of other seasonal rangers to say anything. Two of them, Mountaineers members Bill Brockman and Carsten Lien, went to the club's conservation committee for assistance. A joint committee representing several environmental organizations was created, and included Polly Dyer, conservation committee chairwoman; Chester Powell, Mountaineers president; Patrick Goldsworthy, representing the Sierra Club; Emily Haig, representing the Audubon Society; John Osseward, representing Olympic Park Associates; and Philip Zalesky, vice president of the Federation of Western Outdoor Clubs. All were members of The Mountaineers.

The night their report was presented to the conservation committee, all the members agreed to send the following telegram to the director of the National Park Service: "Request immediate cessation of logging operations in Olympic National Park pending confidential investigation of possible irregularities into logging park timber."

Without saying it outright, the telegram suggested a suspicion of graft. It was a political bombshell and got immediate results because the 1956 presidential campaign was in full swing. The National Park Service director met with the joint committee, and when pressed on the issue declared, "The National Park Service has taken a calculated risk. There will be no further logging in Olympic National Park."

STATE PARKS

The Mountaineers played a pivotal role in the creation of Washington's system of state parks. Two figures stand out in this effort, Robert Moran and Edward Allen.

Moran, an early club member, had been mayor of Seattle during the Great Fire of 1889 and was the owner of Moran Shipyards. He had a palatial home on Orcas Island in the San Juans and had acquired thousands of acres of land on the island, including Mount Constitution. Moran retired to his Orcas Island home after his doctors gave him but a short time to live, though he was to defy their diagnosis and live considerably longer.

Since Moran could no longer come to The Mountaineers, he invited them to come to him. On the fourth annual San Juan–Orcas Island Labor Day outing, 106 club members "enjoyed the never-failing Moran hospitality and the ever-inviting Mount Constitution panoramas."

Moran reminded his guests that he was ready to turn his property over to the state for use as a park, though he hadn't been able to get the state to accept it. The Mountaineers therefore began to promote the idea. A State Parks Commission

had been established in 1914 and had accepted the deeds to Larrabee State Park south of Bellingham and to some historic acreage near Toledo in southwest Washington. But the commission received no encouragement from the governor and took no further action to establish more parks.

The public was almost completely unaware of the commission because of its inactivity. The panel included Governor Louis Hart as chairman, several other elected state officials, and one representative of the public. Edward Allen, an assistant state attorney general and later longtime vice president of The Mountaineers, was secretary to the commission. Allen finally brought about a meeting of the commission in order to present Moran's offer, but when it was made, Hart replied: "We can't take it. We haven't the power to take it. I'm hearing nothing more about this."

Hart's refusal apparently was based on his belief that the state could not afford to maintain a system of parks, and at any rate should not be in the business of owning any more land than was necessary.

After that, Hart refused to call another meeting of the commission, and in 1920 he abolished it. In its place, the legislature established a three-man State Park Board, which excluded the governor at his own request. Allen, using his considerable political skills, persuaded the new board to accept the deed to Moran's property. When the governor was informed that same day, he was furious. Allen was called in and told to take the deed back. "The title has passed to the state of Washington," he replied coolly. "There is nothing that can be done about it."

When the park was dedicated the following year, Hart took full credit for the acceptance of Moran's Orcas Island property. Allen was

Robert Moran (center), a retired shipbuilder and former Seattle mayor, donated land on Orcas Island for a state park. When the governor refused it, he and other club members worked successfully to have the deed accepted. The action spurred further interest in state parks and led to the formation of parks that today are enjoyed by millions of people every year. Photo: Asahel Curtis, Special Collections, University of Washington Libraries, neg. no. 7241.

conspicuously absent from the ceremony, the governor having failed to invite him. Nevertheless, this act by Moran and Allen gave impetus to what is today a system of state parks renowned for their beauty and diversity.

The Mountaineers is still active in establishing state parks, including Peshastin Pinnacles State Park in 1991 near Leavenworth. The club led the effort to buy the land from a rancher, who had closed it to climbing for liability reasons.

The land was then presented to the state, which maintains it specifically for rock climbing.

MOUNT RAINIER NATIONAL PARK

If there is one landmark in which The Mountaineers has taken a special interest, it is Mount Rainier. In the beginning, there was much agitation to make the mountain more accessible, with roads leading to the park and trails

Joe Hazard, a club member from 1911 to 1965 and shown here during the 1923 outing to Mount Garibaldi in British Columbia, was chief guide at Mount Rainier in 1919 and 1920. He dreamed of a trail extending from Alaska to the tip of South America and personally sited and helped build portions of the Cascade Crest Trail (now part of the Pacific Crest Trail, which runs from Canada to Mexico) in Washington State. Hazard authored the pioneering books The Pacific Crest Trail *and* Snow Sentinels of the Pacific Northwest.
Photo: Ralph Dyer, Special Collections, University of Washington Libraries, neg. no. 18135.

within it. The club's outings in these early years pioneered portions of the Wonderland Trail around the mountain. After roads and trails were built, there came a desire to protect the aesthetic qualities of the approaches. The effort to preserve the forest strip along the Chinook Highway (State Route 410) is an example.

Two efforts made by The Mountaineers in the 1920s were of significant national importance. In 1928, Edward Allen prepared a statement for The Mountaineers that advocated setting aside wilderness areas within the park. This was a proposal that preceded the National Wilderness Act by many decades. Allen was to report later that the Department of the Interior acted on this proposal by designating several areas in Mount Rainier National Park as wilderness territory: Ipsut Pass, areas north of Berry Peak, Spray Park, Mystic Lake, Yakima Park, St. Andrew's Park, and Indian Henry's Hunting Ground. They were listed as areas to be free from roads, hotels, pay camps, or other commercial developments, but open for hiking and horse travel. This move contributed to the direction that the National Park Service took for all the nation's parks.

The second national precedent came with establishing the idea that national parks belong to the public and not to the federal bureaucracy that controls them. In 1922, the Rainier National Park Company, the concessionaire that had been granted a monopoly on park services by National Park Service Director Stephen Mather, informed the Tacoma branch of the club that it could not use private trucks to cross park land.

A group from Tacoma had planned a three-day Labor Day weekend outing from a point about four miles inside the park boundary. They had rented a van and a small truck to haul their gear, but were forced by the Park Service to unload their gear at the park boundary, load it onto a similar truck provided by the concessionaire, and walk the four miles by road while their rented van slowly followed them. Upon return they had to repeat the process in reverse. "This was a comedy worthy of being filmed," a Mountaineers report concluded.

By the end of the year, club members had organized to fight this corruption and mounted a nationwide attack on the Park Service. Forming a special committee to document the activities of the Rainier National Park Company, The Mountaineers distributed its report to every member of Congress and to every park-using group in the country. A subsequent lawsuit filed by Seattle attorney and club member George Wright helped establish the public's right of ownership and brought an end to Mather's practice of assigning monopolies in the parks without competitive bidding.

A BRIEF HIATUS

During the Depression and World War II, The Mountaineers' dedication to conservation issues waned as other matters became more pressing. Membership fell off during the 1930s, and for the first time the club actively recruited new members. The explosion in climbing that occurred following the advent of the climbing course in 1935 also served to siphon energy away from conservation issues.

Finally, World War II sent the club into a conservation hiatus, during which period its main contribution was to provide men and women to staff the fire lookouts in the mountains. This proved to be much more important than anyone thought at the time because Japanese submarines were surfacing off the coast and sending up balloons with incendiary devices in an attempt to start massive wildfires and thereby divert manpower from the war effort.

Art Winder, shown during the 1944 summer outing, single-handedly conducted The Mountaineers conservation efforts during the 1930s and 1940s. His call to action was not heard until the 1950s, when the club once again began to be active in environmental issues, taking up arms against such proposals as a tramway to the top of Mount Rainier. Photo: Mabel Furry, Special Collections, University of Washington Libraries, neg. no. 18140.

Those who were on the lookouts suspected as much at the time, but it couldn't be proven until long after the war when Japanese documents were made public.

From the 1930s to the 1960s, the club retreated to a defensive posture on environmental issues, but a few remarkable individuals kept the momentum going.

Beginning in 1926, Joseph Hazard worked to create Washington's Cascade Crest Trail as part of the Pacific Crest Trail system. He tirelessly explored much of the mountain terrain to site the trail and worked closely with the Forest Service to carry out the project. By 1939 the trail had been cut from the Columbia River to the Canadian border, although the last splice for the entire Pacific Crest Trail, an easement across private land in California, wasn't completed until 1993. Perhaps Hazard's dream of a trail extending all the way from Alaska to the tip of South America may yet be realized.

Another notable effort was led by Stuart Hertz and John and Chris Lehmann of the Everett branch when they formed the Glacier Peak Association in 1927 to preserve the timbered valleys in the Cascades, especially the Whitechuck Valley. Also, the branch was one of the few groups to express delight in a proposal by Secretary of the Interior Harold Ickes for a Great Cascade Ice Park, a project that unfortunately never gained sufficient momentum.

It wasn't until after World War II that the club again took up the conservation cause in a committed way. Art Winder, who during the 1940s had been something of a lone voice crying out in the wilderness, reminded members of the club's conservation ideals in an article in the 1950 annual, asking, "Will we be too late? . . . Complacency is not a virtue for the preservationists."

Winder's call for action came just in time, for

in 1953, Washington Governor Arthur Langlie appointed an Olympic National Park Review Committee to study the park's boundaries. The Mountaineers was able to expand the committee, which was initially made up almost entirely of industrial interests. Although the committee's majority report recommended further study, The Mountaineers generated an outpouring of letters opposing deletion of portions of Olympic National Park, and Langlie stopped pushing for a reduction of the park boundaries.

One of the club members appointed to attend meetings of the Park Review Committee was Polly Dyer, at that time secretary of the club's conservation committee. For the next forty years and more, she would prove to be an exceptional conservation advocate. An example of her tenacity came in 1974 when, as part of a political compromise that extended the Olympic Wilderness Coastline to Point of the Arches, the north shore of Lake Quinault was to be removed from Olympic National Park. Dyer and Philip Zalesky kept the issue alive, exploiting every avenue of leverage until the U.S. Supreme Court ruled in an unrelated case that the political maneuvering on which the land swap was based was unconstitutional. Members of Rep. Lloyd Meeds' staff, who had written the legislation, expressed disbelief that Dyer and Zalesky, working alone, had been able to save two thousand acres of virgin forest.

The misguided wilderness development efforts of the 1950s not only had the effect of reenergizing the club's conservation efforts but also of spreading the conservation base in the Northwest at large. One of the more outrageous plans was a move to promote tourism at Mount Rainier National Park by building a funicular tramway to the top of the mountain, a deluxe lodge at Paradise Valley, a swimming pool, and a golf course on Paradise Valley's flowered meadows. It was another scheme by Governor Langlie's office to obtain federal aid.

Led by The Mountaineers, conservationists fought such desecration of a national park. In open hearings where the public was invited to testify, state officials were shocked to find that the plan's opponents were far more numerous and vociferous than development advocates. Letters from the public ran 10-to-1 against the tramway.

Winder, whose 1950 call had aroused the old passions once again, considered this a turning point in Northwest environmental efforts. It meant that politicians were beginning to wake up to the fact that conservation had serious political implications.

THE CONSERVATION RESURGENCE

After reawakening in the 1950s, The Mountaineers again became a major player in wilderness preservation. Richard Brooks initiated an effort in 1953 to secure the Glacier Peak Wilderness. The subsequent struggle with the Forest Service eventually led to the big push to establish North Cascades National Park, and the Glacier Peak Wilderness followed later. The park had long been sought, and The Mountaineers helped form the North Cascades Conservation Council to promote the idea. In 1958, club directors formally voted to support the park and joined with the council to present a prospectus.

When asked to give his support to the park, Washington Senator Henry M. Jackson, chairman of the Senate Interior Committee, replied, "You get up the parade, and I'll lead it."

Members of The Mountaineers became heavily involved in the publicity blitz that followed. For example, Harvey and Betty Manning took over the North Cascades Conservation Council publication, renamed it *The Wild Cascades*, and under them it became one of the liveliest conservation publications in the nation.

Manning was editor of *Mountaineering: The Freedom of the Hills*, the climbing textbook first published by The Mountaineers in 1960. Money from that book, which had been invested in a special publication fund, was used in 1964 to develop the book *The North Cascades*, a view of the mountains from a climber's perspective, with text by Harvey Manning and photos by Tom Miller. *The North Cascades* was one of the first books to open the public's eyes to the great natural beauty of the region and was distributed around the nation with the help of the Sierra Club.

In 1965, Sierra Club leader David Brower, who also was a member of The Mountaineers, prevailed on Manning to rush out a fact manual on behalf of the North Cascades park proposal. Instead, Manning wrote a series of impassioned essays, published as a book by the Sierra Club, titled *The Wild Cascades: Forgotten Parkland*, which contained some of the finest nature writing the Northwest had ever seen.

Club member Patrick Goldsworthy, a University of Washington biochemistry professor who headed the North Cascades Conservation Council, led his troops through public hearings and intensive lobbying. At one House of Representatives Interior Committee hearing at the Benjamin Franklin Hotel in Seattle, eight hundred people lined up to testify. Most were Mountaineers members. The North Cascades National Park Act finally was signed by President Lyndon Johnson in 1968.

The Mountaineers also aided passage of the National Wilderness Act of 1964, when the club was called on to help organize and lead a series of Northwest Wilderness Conferences. The first of these was held in Portland, with The Mountaineers playing a vital role before a national audience of conservation leaders. At the conference banquet, Philip Zalesky showed slides of the proposed Glacier Peak Wilderness and urged national support for The Mountaineers' efforts. But the highlight of that banquet was Howard Zahniser, the father of the Wilderness Act and executive director of the Wilderness Society, sharing for the first time anywhere the language of the wilderness bill he had drafted for Senator Hubert Humphrey.

Then came the effort to gain federal protection for the Alpine Lakes area, which had become practically a backyard wilderness for The Mountaineers because it was only an hour's drive from Seattle and Everett. John Warth urged preservation of this area with articles in the club bulletin and in other conservation publications. His was a lonely battle, since everyone else seemed to be immersed in the North Cascades National Park battle. But he wasn't entirely alone. It was about that time that Brock Evans appeared in the Pacific Northwest.

Evans, an Easterner, had reportedly told his fiancée, "Darling, before we get married, I have to tell you something. When we get married, you will have to live in Seattle." She seems to have accepted the shock of his announcement, and thus the newly graduated lawyer arrived in Seattle, his only other experience with the city having been a visit on one summer weekend.

Evans and his wife joined The Mountaineers almost immediately, and not long after were sitting atop a peak in the Snoqualmie Pass area when Evans, with Eastern naïveté, asked a fellow Mountaineer about a bare spot on the side of a mountain in the distance. "That's a clear-cut," came the answer. "Can the Forest Service really do that?" Evans asked incredulously.

∞

Patrick Goldsworthy, an honorary member of the club, shakes hands with President Lyndon Johnson after the bill creating North Cascades National Park was signed in 1968. Goldsworthy, a biochemistry professor and president of the North Cascades Conservation Council, assembled vast quantities of data that argued in favor of creating the park. He was also instrumental in the establishment of many wilderness areas in the state. Photo: The Mountaineers *annual, 1969.*

That experience led Evans to volunteer for the club's conservation division, and he cut his political teeth forming a speakers bureau on behalf of the proposed North Cascades National Park. Evans went on to become a founding member of the Washington Environmental Council, and in 1997 was vice president of the national Audubon Society and that group's Washington, D.C., lobbyist.

A decision by club directors in 1971 to publish another book, *The Alpine Lakes,* led directly to establishment of the wilderness area. The book was written by Brock Evans and edited by Harvey Manning, with photos by Ed Cooper and Bob Gunning. Norman Winn, testifying on behalf of The Mountaineers in the nation's capital, presented copies of the book to every member of the Senate committee.

After much lobbying, President Gerald Ford received the bill establishing the wilderness area. But along with it came advice from the Department of Agriculture, the Department of

Harvey Manning on Mount Persis in 1951. A prolific author and dedicated conservationist, Manning in his early days with the club was just another rag-tag peak bagger. Photo: Chuck Allyn.

Commerce, and the Office of Management and Budget to veto it. The Forest Service even drafted veto language for the president.

At that point, Washington State Governor Dan Evans (no relation to Brock Evans) borrowed the book from a friend and took it with him to the White House to show the president.

As reporter Timothy Egan later wrote in the *New York Times*: "Gerald Ford was finally persuaded as president to set aside nearly 40,000 acres of the Alpine Lakes Wilderness an hour east of Seattle after being shown a picture book on the area. It touched something in Mr. Ford from his days as a Boy Scout."

Another Mountaineers book by Manning was influential in passage of the Washington State Wilderness Act of 1984, when the state's senators and congressmen were all sent copies of *Washington Wilderness: The Unfinished Work,* with photos by Pat O'Hara.

The Washington State Wilderness Act actually resulted from efforts of the Forest Service and the forest products industry to stem the tide of wilderness designations. The Mountaineers joined with sixteen other organizations to form the Washington Wilderness Coalition to protect wilderness interests. Joanne Roberts, chairwoman of the club's Conservation Division, and Winn, an attorney, worked with the Washington Wilderness Coalition, and Rick Rutz provided the forest analysis that played such a significant role in the final outcome. What could have been a political disaster instead led to protection for an additional million acres of wilderness.

Rutz, with his technically trained mind, was also the one who came up with the idea of tearing down two dams on the Elwha River, one of which is in Olympic National Park, as a means of returning once-great salmon spawning areas to their original condition. His work spurred organization of a coalition of Northwest conservationists and an Indian tribe. Congress in 1992 passed the Elwha Restoration Act. The funding to remove the dams was still pending in 1997, although one powerful opponent, Republican U.S. Senator Slade Gorton, of Washington, decided in the face of public pressure to go along with removal of at least one of them. Rutz has more recently been involved in encouraging the Northwest Power Council to commit to energy conservation and wildlife protection.

The Mountaineers has also struggled on behalf of Mount St. Helens National Volcanic Monument, the Columbia River Gorge National Scenic Area, and the Olympic Coast National Marine Sanctuary. The club has supported the Endangered Species Act and joined in lawsuits to preserve the last of the state's ancient forests.

Not to be forgotten among the successes is one that is largely unheralded. A great many trails had been built in the Cascades and Olympics in the 1930s by the Civilian Conservation Corps, most for fire protection purposes. After World War II, many became obsolete, and the Forest Service abandoned them. Others were wiped out as logging plunged deeper into the mountains, obliterating the trails with a maze of roads. Club members Harvey Manning, Ira Spring, Louise Marshall, and Ruth Ittner began a campaign to halt this loss of trails.

Manning and Spring authored the *100 Hikes* and *Footsore* series of trail guides, published by the club, which have educated countless hikers to conservation efforts in the Northwest. Marshall co-authored the first of the guides with Manning and later founded *Signpost*, a magazine to keep hikers apprised of trail changes. Ittner has kept the conservation division aware of trail needs, and with Marshall and others formed the Washington Trails Association, which continues to publish *Signpost*.

Just as the first club outings spread the conservation message to the public, so today's club-published trail guides introduce more hikers to the conservation ethic than perhaps any other effort by The Mountaineers.

The club's innovative Conservation for Kids program for schools has helped turn students on to an ecological ethic. The club sends a presenter to schools that want to participate. The presenter shows up at a classroom or assembly without warning and instantly launches into an entertaining environmental spiel. In

costume, the character leads students through a give-and-take presentation that typically lasts forty-five minutes to an hour.

First-grade students get Old John, an elderly gent who tells stories of a time when there was less waste than today. Older students get Archie Mattox, a former logger with an environmental bent. Both characters have been played by Loren Foss, the head of the club's Conservation Division, who is a certified teacher with professional acting experience.

While the club can count many accomplishments in conservation, working with the club also has led to frustration for some members. Irving Clark, the early environmental leader, tired of its ponderous decision-making process in the 1920s and distanced himself from further club efforts. He went on to become a founding member of The Wilderness Society. Many other individuals have started out with club efforts, then gone on to organize more specific programs on behalf of the environment. The Mountaineers has always been important as a nurturing ground for getting people started in conservation.

And it must be mentioned that not all members agree with the preservation clause written into the club constitution. Certainly, Asahel Curtis didn't, and some later board members actively opposed club efforts on behalf of the environment. Overall, however, the trend is toward embracing the philosophy and working toward fulfillment of preservation goals.

∞

Left: Mountain and high-country photographs taken by twin brothers Bob and Ira Spring influenced hundreds of thousands of people who saw them in national publications and helped sway public sentiment toward wilderness preservation. Ira, co-author with Harvey Manning of the 100 Hikes and Footsore series of trail guides, was recently named an honorary member of the club and remains deeply involved in trail conservation efforts. Shown on a 1950 climbing trip are Bob, Pat (married to Ira), Norma (married to Bob), and Ira Spring.
Photo: Ira Spring.

∞

Above: Morris Moen, shown here receiving The Mountaineers Service Award in 1969, joined the club in 1952. A founding member of The Mountaineers Foundation in 1968 and its president (or chairman) from 1971 to 1990, he has also been very involved with the Players drama group and the Rhododendron Preserve on the Kitsap Peninsula.
Photo: Lynn Moen.

Norman Winn has been a member of the Conservation Division for twenty-five years and its chairman on two separate occasions. While club president in 1976, he lobbied Congress for passage of the bill creating the Alpine Lakes Wilderness and in 1984 lobbied again for the Washington Wilderness Act. He has written many of The Mountaineers' position papers, particularly those on forestry and salmon issues. Winn has also been an active climb leader over that same period. Many of his climbs and outings have been in the North Cascades, where he has a number of first ascents. Photo: Norm Winn

THE MOUNTAINEERS FOUNDATION

The Mountaineers Foundation is an independent organization founded in 1968 after the club's tax-exempt status was revoked for a brief period by the Internal Revenue Service. Relying entirely on contributions, it makes annual grants to organizations in the Pacific Northwest that work to protect air and water quality, wetlands, wild rivers and Puget Sound, endangered species, and natural areas. The foundation has helped fund such efforts as wetlands preservation along the Snohomish River, rehabilitation of the Schurman Rock climbing facility at Camp Long in West Seattle, studies on the effects of boating on killer whales, and a new map of the Alpine Lakes Wilderness. It also donates to jointly shared projects with the club, including the Conservation for Kids program.

Under Mountaineers President Jesse Epstein, the board of trustees approved the formation of the foundation as a tax-exempt organization, and articles of incorporation were filed with the state in June 1968. The seven incorporators—Epstein, John Davis, Leo Gallagher, Joan Hansen, Morris Moen, John Osseward, and Paul Wiseman—all had been officers or trustees of the club at one time, and they elected Epstein first president of the foundation.

Foundation bylaws do not restrict membership to members of The Mountaineers, but do specify that a majority of trustees be club members. In 1997, seven past presidents were among the nineteen board members.

The goals of The Mountaineers Foundation can be summed up by the first sentence of its vision statement: "Dedicated to passing the best possible environmental legacy to ensuing generations."

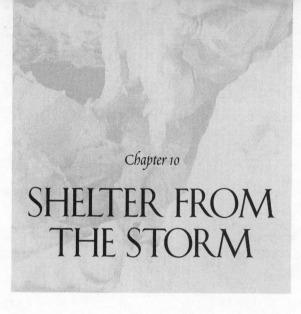

Chapter 10

SHELTER FROM
THE STORM

Some of The Mountaineers' biggest adventures had nothing to do with the outdoors. They came from the on-again, off-again search for a clubhouse, a permanent place to meet.

The Mountaineers' first meeting place was at the Seattle Chamber of Commerce hall downtown, where the club continued to gather for ten years. Then, in September 1917, members realized a dream and rented their own rooms at the Central Building. Unfortunately, membership was falling off after the early years of growth, and the monthly meetings were soon rotating once again through various Seattle meeting halls: the YWCA, the Merchant's Exchange, the Women's University Club, the Masonic Lodge, and the new Chamber of Commerce auditorium in the Arctic Building.

It wasn't until 1930 that the club settled more or less permanently into rooms at the Rialto Building. It was in this building that Wolf Bauer first rappelled down the open stairwell to the marble floor below while climbing course students lined the rickety wooden railings to watch. But in 1942, soon after the United States entered World War II, the USO pushed the club out of the Rialto Building so it

could use the space for entertaining soldiers and sailors.

The club next landed at 523½ Pike Street, just above the Green Apple Pie Cafe. The rooms there were spacious and affordable, with an area for small meetings as well as for the club's growing collection of books and other reference material. Lectures for the climbing course and other large-scale activities were conducted in a succession of rented auditoriums. For a number of years, the Pike Street clubrooms were presided over by the sole employee of that time, a part-time secretary.

Lloyd Anderson eventually moved his fledgling Recreational Equipment Cooperative down the hall, thereby establishing a kind of Mountaineers Central. The club and the co-op soon became identified as one, with the co-op commonly referred to as "The Mountaineers Co-op," even though there was no direct relationship between the club and the co-op.

Starting in 1954, a succession of special committees conducted a search that ended up spanning eleven years, looking for affordable space to handle the growing club's needs. In 1965, a two-story building at 715–19 Pike

In the late 1960s the club moved to 715–19 Pike Street. The clubrooms were directly above the Caballero tavern, and noise and rowdiness often disrupted night meetings. The Pike Street location was a prime downtown property, and the club was eventually forced out to make way for the Washington State Convention and Trade Center. Photo: Tom Green, Mountaineers Books collection.

Street was selected. Its main asset was a sizable auditorium, which ironically had been used by the USO during the war. Among the negative factors was that the clubroom and auditorium were on the second floor, with a restaurant and tavern directly below. Board members had hoped to get away from the taverns that lined Pike Street.

The Mountaineers bought the building for eighty thousand dollars and in 1968, after much renovation, moved in. The board learned to live with the tavern music that drifted up from below, and eventually the young Mountaineers Books operation also moved into the space. For a time, some board members would arrive at meetings early so they could claim the chairs closest to the window. If the meeting grew a little dull, they could always look across the street into the windows of the Soft Touch body painting studio. The club remained at that site for fifteen years without further discussion of moving, and might still be there if the property hadn't been so desirable for development.

But on December 27, 1982, the ax began to fall. Club officials were advised that the proposed Washington State Convention and Trade Center was considering a freeway lid on Pike Street as one of three potential sites. This would require taking over most of The Mountaineers property.

The state proposed to offer "fair market value," but that amount was far less than its actual resale value, and the convention center threatened condemnation if The Mountaineers refused to sell. Convention center developers quickly obtained permission to buy out all adjacent property owners, leaving The Mountaineers as the lone holdout.

President Errol Nelson wrote to the convention center, outlining The Mountaineers' requirements for selling: It could incur no capital debt or mortgage costs; future operating costs could not measurably exceed present operating costs; if temporary relocation were necessary, these expenses would be paid by the convention center.

The letter was ignored. Nelson was forced to report back to the club that the convention center apparently assumed there was no reason to listen to The Mountaineers because they could simply condemn the property. The club needed a heavyweight in the ring to slug it out for them.

John Davis weighed in. An attorney and past club president, Davis wrote to the chairman of the Washington State Convention and Trade Center Commission on February 16, 1983, advising him that if the center chose the freeway site it should be prepared to leave the club's property alone. Copies were sent to every member of the commission. This was no idle warning from a minor downtown lawyer but a shot across the bow from a high-powered gun. Many of the people Davis contacted were long-standing friends and knew his abilities in court. A prolonged fight could hold up the convention center, which was on a fast track.

The commission responded quickly, saying the input of The Mountaineers was important, but it was still considering which site to choose. However, when Nelson asked to present the findings of an architect hired by the club to explore building options, he was granted only five minutes at the next meeting.

At about this time, Davis was joined by one of the most unlikely allies in the long history of the club, downtown developer Martin Selig. A new club member, Selig had agreed to become part of the negotiating team for The Mountaineers. Suddenly, the convention center found itself in a fair fight. Everybody knew Selig, who had a reputation for shrewd bargaining and courtroom dogfights from which he seemed to emerge unscathed.

Just as suddenly, an attorney for the convention center called Davis and asked for permission to negotiate on behalf of The Mountaineers to sell the club property in a complex real estate transaction in which the developer would purchase the property for resale to the convention center. Since the developer already owned most of the other property in the area, all would be sold together as a package deal.

The hitch was that the offer was for only $200 per square foot. The Mountaineers had looked at the Norway Center near the Seattle waterfront as the most practical clubhouse site available, and the club needed $278 per square foot, or $2 million, for its property in order to buy the Norway Center. Selig sat down with Davis and the convention center attorney to spell out The Mountaineers' position.

The club prepared its own offer of $2 million in cash for the Norway Center, contingent on being able to negotiate the sale of its Pike Street building by an August 15 deadline. Nelson advised the convention center and its lawyers that if negotiations were not completed by that date, The Mountaineers "probably would be content to stay at its present site" and hold up the convention center in court.

After complex negotiations, The Mountaineers agreed to sell its property to the developer for $2,065,000, with the developer to pay the club's moving costs. The Mountaineers assigned its right to purchase the Norway Center to the developer, which was to buy the Norway Center for the club, then let the title pass directly to The Mountaineers. This complicated real estate agreement, which could only have been thought up by people with long experience in downtown property transactions, closed on September 8, 1983.

The Seattle Weekly newspaper summed up the negotiations on September 28: "Sidelight on Washington State Convention Center negotiations: It pays to know with whom you're dealing. A few months ago, Convention Center types were rather loudly offering to cajole, legally condemn or bully The Mountaineers into giving up their little clubhouse on the center site. Then the venerable outdoor group brought in its own pair of negotiator members: skyscraper king Martin Selig and high-powered attorney John Davis from Davis, Wright, Todd, Riese and Jones. The Mountaineers are now happily settling into a newly purchased home at the Norway Center."

The Mountaineers clubhouse remains at the former Norway Center at 300 Third Avenue West. Rather than having a single auditorium, the building has a series of auditoriums of varying size, so different groups can meet at the same time. The club has remodeled the lower section of the building to house its administrative offices and bookstore, and rents unused space to other organizations for meetings.

GROWTH YEARS

The Mountaineers' growth has been generally steady, with exceptions such as a dip about ten years after the club's formation and another during the Great Depression, when few people could afford the dues or the cost of equipment. But membership growth seldom has reflected the much greater growth in activities.

The constitution and bylaws adopted in 1906 defined the duties of only four standing committees—Outings, House, Program, and Publications—but allowed the president to appoint "other special committees as may be needed."

These committees flourished when needed or withered as members went on to new interests. For example, the years following World War II saw exceptional growth, with membership jumping to 3,540 in 195 6, and the number of committees reporting to the board climbing accordingly, to thirty-four in 1955.

Starting in the mid-1950s, it became apparent that the club was expanding beyond its ability to manage itself under the old structure. The watershed year was 1957, when President Paul Wiseman promoted a plan for the creation of divisions, with each committee assigned to one of the divisions. Committees with like interests and problems were put in the same division. Each division's leadership was to include one or two trustees and one or more others, who would meet regularly with the chairs of their division's committees. By the end of 1957, four divisions were operating—Administrative, Properties, Outdoor, and Indoor. Two more, Publications and Conservation, were being formed.

In 1967, after years of debate, the board decided that a business manager should be hired in place of the longtime clubroom secretary, and that dues should be increased to support such professional administration. Edward "Ted" Murray resigned as club treasurer to become the club's half-time paid accountant, and later Howard Stansbury succeeded him as business manager. The position eventually became full-time.

Stansbury retired as business manager in 1981, and Sue Justen replaced him. She immediately became involved in remodeling the Pike Street clubrooms to alleviate a space crunch, then led the club through the traumatic building swap that followed. However, the move to the Norway Center in 1983 brought far larger operational costs, and an attempt to manage a restaurant that had been inherited with the

building turned out to be another cash drain. The cost of liability insurance also had begun to soar, aggravating the club's financial problems, and additional funds were desperately needed for the conservation and outdoor recreation battles brought on by the policies of President Reagan's administration, which sought to open wilderness areas to commercial development.

To make up for a running deficit, the club's general fund was drawn down to the point of depletion. A reserve fund was needed for unforeseen expenses, lawsuits, and any natural disasters that might affect club property. The move to the Norway Center had raised the stakes on all counts.

The resolution came when the board closed the restaurant and launched a study of the reasons why the club was spending beyond its means. An outside accounting firm, Touche Ross, was hired to come up with a balanced budget plan, and the board dedicated itself to developing a business arrangement that would deter it from getting into this fix again.

Touche Ross advised that any decisions to raise dues and fees should be established by the board based on business considerations, and not put to a vote of the membership, as the club's bylaws at that time required. "It is our experience that non-profits in which dues are voted on by the membership run into serious financial problems because dues increases become an emotional issue rather than a sound financial business issue," the accounting experts told the board. A committee went to work on changing the bylaws, and in October 1987 committee members approved a revision to require the board of trustees to determine dues and fees. The new bylaws, designed to enable club officers and the board to deal more quickly and effectively with financial crises, were approved by a vote of the full club membership in February 1989.

Another aspect of the financial plan was the change from a business manager to an executive director to run the club. Sue Justen resigned as business manager in early 1988, and Virginia Felton was hired as executive director. Felton had been director of property management and marketing at the Pike Place Market, and brought with her valuable knowledge about renting out rooms, which was the main financial hope in managing the large new building.

The club's financial situation began to improve, and on June 5, 1992, The Mountaineers hand-carried a check for $106,639 to Pacific First Federal Savings Bank, paying off in its entirety a loan the club had taken out to help it through the period of difficulty. Though the loan was small in comparison to the overall value of club assets, officers and members alike always had been uncomfortable with carrying any debt at all. By 1993, the treasurer could report that all areas of the club were financially sound and doing well, and the financial crisis had been weathered.

In January 1997, Virginia Felton resigned as executive director. She was succeeded by Suzanne D. Weckerly, who had extensive experience in corporate planning and working with volunteers in nonprofit organizations. Weckerly served as executive director until March 1998. As this book goes to press, the search for a new executive director is about to begin.

Chapter 11

BRANCHING OUT

The main Seattle group of The Mountaineers that was formed in 1906 wasn't alone for long. An informal auxiliary group got under way in nearby Everett in 1910, and in 1911 became the club's first official branch.

The Mountaineers today has branches in four Washington towns on the west side of the Cascade Mountains—Bellingham, Everett, Olympia, and Tacoma—and in Wenatchee on the east side. Branches that formed in Monroe in 1914 and Bremerton in 1921 lapsed from sparse membership.

Each of the five semiautonomous branches has its own focus, depending on local interests, and its own opportunities for leadership. It isn't necessary to come to Seattle headquarters for a meeting or activity or to support an environmental cause; the branches have excursions and causes of their own. Each has a representative on the club's board of trustees.

The structure of the club—with most members affiliated with the Seattle location and its activities and central administration, and far fewer members in the branch organizations—is something that came about over time rather than being planned. The situation has both

strengths and weaknesses, and coordination among all the elements of the club is an ongoing challenge.

Club leaders are always looking for ways to achieve economies of scale rather than duplicating efforts or facilities. The various outdoor activities groups coordinate to avoid such environmental problems as sending climbing parties from two locations to the same peak on the same day. The trustees will be looking at a variety of ideas as they plan for the future, such as the possibility of creating a "Seattle branch" distinct from the administrative headquarters, and establishing a new branch on the east side of Lake Washington, across from Seattle.

EVERETT

The Everett branch began with a chance meeting between Asahel Curtis of The Mountaineers and Dr. H. B. Hinman at Mount Rainier in August 1909. Hinman, an Everett dentist, met Curtis at Reese's camp, one of several tent camps set up above Paradise that shifted location from time to time and existed to accommodate summer park visitors. The men fell to talking about their shared passion, the mountains, and

H. B. Hinman, Arthur Gist, and Fred Q. Gorton stop at an old ranger's cabin during the 1914 outing to Mount Stuart. Hinman introduced the concept of branch organizations when he organized the Everett branch in 1910 and got the club to change its bylaws to allow it. Gorton was a frequent summer outing leader.
Photo: Garda Fogg, Special Collections, University of Washington Libraries, neg. no. 18124.

Hinman resolved to become a club member.

"Immediately upon my return . . . I made application for membership, and after being elected the idea occurred to me to secure enough local members so that we might have walks the same as were held in Seattle," Hinman reported in the 1910 annual.

That same year, forty applicants from Everett and five from towns in the vicinity were elected to membership.

At the time, Mountaineers bylaws did not authorize branches, but the club's board accepted Everett as a "tentative" organization. There seems to have been little doubt of its permanence, since the 1910 annual already was referring to it as the Everett Mountaineers. After a new constitution and bylaws were passed in 1911 permitting branches, Everett became an official part of the club.

The branch lost little time getting going. In 1912, it sponsored twenty-two local walks, five of them joint walks with Seattle; two three-day outings, one to Mount Index and the other to Whitehorse Mountain; and stereopticon lectures open to the public free of charge that each drew several hundred people.

Of those local walks, Joan Astell recounted in the 1956 annual: "A typical early trip would find the lady Mountaineer dressed in ankle-length skirts, long-sleeve blouses, a stylish bonnet and oxfords. She would probably be carrying her lunch tied in a red handkerchief as she boarded the boat for Mukilteo and then walked back to Everett, stopping en route to make coffee and roast wieners."

Other popular destinations included Forest Park, Silver Lake, and North Creek, all of which are now developed neighborhoods with the old-growth forests long gone and the streams diverted into culverts, and the Tulalip Indian Reservation. Early transportation included chartered boat to Whidbey Island or horse-drawn wagon to Halls Lake to meet Seattle members arriving at the end of the Interurban rail line. Members could travel into the central Cascades on the Hartford Eastern Gas Car, which operated from 1915 to 1936 and transported ore from the mines at Monte Cristo.

One of the Everett Mountaineers' first ascents, led by H. B. Hinman, was of 6,852-foot Whitehorse Mountain in 1913, a dominating peak that rises 6,000 vertical feet in just three miles from the town of Darrington. They thought it was a first ascent, only to learn much later that it had been climbed in 1909. In 1918, Everett hosted The Mountaineers' highly successful summer outing to the Monte Cristo area, attended by sixty-five club members.

By 1921, the Everett branch was on the lookout for a lodge of its own. That same year, it leased a former timber camp from the Forest Service at Bear Creek, about thirty miles east of Everett on the northeast side of Mount Pilchuck. The previous tenants were shingle bolt cutters who

had been employed by the Black Bear Shingle Company, which went bankrupt and abandoned the property. And by 1925 the Everett Mountaineers also were discussing terminating the lease and the financial drain it imposed. In 1928 the Everett Mountaineers got out of the lodge business.

Everett's climbing instruction had its informal beginning in 1946 with establishment of a basic course under direction of branch chairman Frank Eder. This precursor course ran for two years, with help from Seattle climbing course leaders. In 1954, the Everett climbing committee was formed to present the basic course again, with Kenn Carpenter as chairman.

As the 1950s rolled on, the Everett climbing program recorded several high points. In 1956, Everett Mountaineers completely circled the summit pyramid of Mount Shuksan by traversing the upper portions of the Hanging Glacier, Crystal Glacier, Sulphide Glacier, and Upper Curtis Glacier. The climbers reached the summit via the Sulphide Glacier to complete this remarkable traverse. In 1958, Everett climbers made two Cascade first ascents, of the north face of Three Fingers and the northwest ridge of Kyes Peak.

By 1956, Everett had developed enough of a core group of climbers that it could present the climbing course without any help from Seattle. In 1976 the branch had to limit enrollment for the first time due to demand. In 1977, the intermediate climbing course was first offered, and intermediate students made their mark with a first ascent of the north face of White Chuck Mountain in June 1988.

The Everett Mountaineers became involved in conservation issues early on, when in 1927 Stuart Hertz and brothers John and Chris Lehmann led the branch to form the Glacier Peak Association with the idea of establishing

The committee that organized the 1931 summer outing to Glacier Peak included Everett branch members Paul Gaskell, John Lehmann, and Bert Church. The Everett branch became involved in conservation issues early on, in 1927, when Lehmann, with his brother Chris and Stuart Hertz, led the formation of Glacier Peak Association, with the idea of establishing a national park that included the Whitechuck Valley and Glacier Peak. Photo: Mabel Furry, Special Collections, University of Washington Libraries, neg. no. 18122.

a national park that included the Whitechuck Valley and Glacier Peak. Though the idea was not successful, logging was significantly delayed in the valley.

The Everett branch first recommended establishment of a Cascade National Park in 1936, the forerunner to North Cascades National Park. A renewed interest in conservation was instigated primarily by member Philip Zalesky, starting in about 1954, and in 1962 a conservation committee was formed with Henry Kral as chairman. The Everett branch was significantly involved in the effort to establish North Cascades National Park, which was created in 1968. The conservation committee now concentrates on wetlands and ancient forests, two of the region's most critical environmental concerns.

For the Washington State centennial in 1989, the Everett Mountaineers rebuilt the Mount Pilchuck fire lookout as it had appeared in the 1930s, working from period photographs and information from previous rebuilding efforts. The original building dated from 1921 and had been repaired and remodeled by the branch in 1941 and 1971.

The branch has also taken on many trail maintenance and construction projects, including repair and upkeep of the spectacular Three Fingers lookout and ladder.

TACOMA

Tacoma's "Auxiliary to The Mountaineers" was formed in March 1912 primarily due to the efforts of A. H. Denman, an attorney with a love for photography and the mountains. He was assisted by John B. Flett, a botanist, and J. Harry Weer, a wholesale grocery executive. Weer, Tacoma branch president for seven years, led the club's 1915 summer outing, a hike entirely around Mount Rainier—a route that became known as the Wonderland Trail. Many subsequent summer outings were headed by Tacoma branch leaders.

Members from Tacoma were active in The Mountaineers from its inception. Charles Landes, a teacher at Tacoma High School and brother of Henry Landes, the club's first president, led the first local walk in the Tacoma area, on March 16, 1907. That excursion, from American Lake to Steilacoom, was the club's third outing.

Before the year 1912 ended, the Tacoma

branch had staged a five-day winter outing at Longmire, which became an annual event. The outing was moved to Paradise in 1917, and attendance figures for 1923 show 160 present. These isolated treks, although halted a decade or so later for insurance reasons, were among

A. H. Denman sets up his camera during the 1922 outing. Denman, a pioneer Tacoma lawyer with a love for photography, was largely responsible for the formation of the Tacoma branch in 1912, and under his leadership the branch pioneered winter outings, mostly to nearby Mount Rainier. Photo: Special Collections, University of Washington Libraries, neg. no. 18131.

Clarence Garner, shown in 1923 during his first summer outing, was a longtime Tacoma branch leader. Garner was known for his yodeling, and no outing was officially over until he had sung "The Old Settler's Song" at the last campfire. Photo: A. H. Denman, Special Collections, University of Washington Libraries, neg. no. 18155.

the area's first organized efforts to get into the mountains in winter, and they pioneered the way for the snowshoeing, skiing, and winter mountaineering that would follow.

For more than fifty years, the Tacoma branch had its own retreat at Irish Cabin, near the main channel of the Carbon River along the road to the Carbon River entrance to Mount Rainier National Park. The cabin was built sometime before the turn of the century by a man known only as Mr. Irish, who worked a nearby copper mine, and was later deserted. In April 1926, a group of Tacoma Mountaineers led by Leo Gallagher passed by the cabin and decided to investigate. They found a fairly large building constructed almost entirely of split cedar, including the floor. Gallagher, Harriet Taylor, and W. W. Kilmer determined that, with a little repair work, the cabin could become a Mountaineers home.

During the Depression, the club bought the cabin and eighteen acres for three hundred dollars. However, the area's virgin forest was logged off not long afterward, destroying much of the charm and beauty of the site. A cabin rehabilitation program was begun in the 1940s, and soon nothing was left of the original cabin but the main floor and walls. Bunks for the cabin were paid for by individual members, with the names of the donors stenciled on them, and eventually there were sleeping quarters for sixty.

Before the road to Mowich Lake made the twenty-four Irish Cabin Peaks more accessible, Irish Cabin was the place to stay for hiking and climbing on the north and west side of Mount Rainier. After the road improvements of the 1950s, the Cabin Peaks became popular day trips from Tacoma.

Eventually the chore of keeping the cabin habitable and free of squatters and vandalism became a problem, and in 1978 the branch

tore it down. The property still is used for car camping and for field trips by the climbing course.

Tacoma is the only branch to have its own clubhouse, located at 2302 North 30th Street in Tacoma's historic Old Town area. In the early 1950s, Leo Gallagher located a desirable lot, bought it, and donated it to the club. Spirited discussion followed over the best type of structure to build. The club's board of trustees met in Tacoma in February 1955 to hear the conflicting views of branch members, and then directed that a questionnaire be sent to all branch members to get their preferences. Finally, an architect was hired to draw up plans.

Volunteers worked on construction for more than a year before the building was ready to be occupied, and the club held its first meeting there in March 1957. Finishing work continued for several years. There was no central heating at first, and members often came to meetings in their climbing clothes to stay warm.

During the 1960s, volunteers under the leadership of John Simac built a twenty-foot-high rock pylon in the walled-in garden behind the clubhouse, hauling the stones from a Renton quarry. Much of the labor for this practice climbing rock was provided by members active in mountain safety, including volunteers from the climbing course, the Tacoma unit of the Mountain Rescue Council, and the Junior Mountaineers. The rock is a neighborhood landmark, used regularly by course participants and members who want to hone their techniques.

OLYMPIA

Origins of the Olympia branch go back to 1963 when Paul Wiseman, a former club president, tallied up the number of members who lived in the area and came up with more than forty,

Paul Wiseman in 1951 on the summer outing to the Olympics. Wiseman, who helped form the Olympia branch, began hiking as a Boy Scout in the 1930s and is still active in hiking and scrambling. He has long been committed to conservation efforts and was one of the seven incorporators of The Mountaineers Foundation in 1968. Photo: Paul Wiseman collection.

most of whom were graduates of the basic climbing course. That was just about the right number, he realized, to act as faculty in a climbing course.

Wiseman and several others organized a Mountaineers climbing course in Olympia that took on thirty-nine students, with Bart Burns as chairman. Wiseman was in charge of the lectures and Gerald Hoyer organized most of the climbs. At the time, club membership was not required before enrolling in the climbing course, and the majority of students weren't Mountaineers. But most of the twenty-six who graduated joined the club, swelling the ranks of members in the lower Puget Sound region and leading Wiseman and others to think about forming an Olympia branch.

The branch was officially created by the board of trustees in September 1963, with Wiseman as chairman and a nucleus of sixty-seven members and one activity: the climbing course. Membership has since grown to more than seven hundred, and there are a dozen different activities.

The branch's conservation efforts include helping establish Wallace Falls State Park near Monroe and forming a wilderness ethics committee to incorporate standards adopted by the club into branch courses.

BELLINGHAM

The Bellingham branch was formed in February 1983 after more than seventy people showed up at a meeting in response to fliers posted around the northern Washington town. Within a month of being created, the branch had bylaws and officers, and a few hikes and scrambles on the calendar. The group has since expanded into climbing, kayaking, rafting, sailing, world travel, and activities focusing on history and geology.

The branch's first instructional class was in scrambling, offered in spring 1985. A climbing course was added in 1987, led by Ken Wilcox and Karen Neubauer. The climbing course continues to fill up each year, with a long waiting list.

In June 1990 the branch began presenting public hiking seminars. Topics such as mountaineering common sense and the purposes and activities of the club are covered in an annual information meeting for the public. Conservation efforts include participation in the Cascade Pass revegetation project and the Adopt-a-Trail group. A main focus has been work on the Bay-to-Baker Trail, which runs from Bellingham Bay to Mount Baker.

WENATCHEE

Interest in establishing a branch in Wenatchee surfaced in summer 1995 after two members who had been active in The Mountaineers, Doug Taylor and Patrick DeVries, moved east of the mountains. They were among organizers of an information meeting in mid-September that drew fifty people, some already Mountaineers members.

Approved by the board of trustees in December 1995 with a membership of seventeen, the Wenatchee branch had about eighty-five members as of 1998. Its activities include courses in basic climbing and mountain scrambling and a wilderness introduction seminar.

Chapter 12

SPREADING THE WORD

From the start, Mountaineers sought to share their experiences with others. This was fitting for an organization heavily influenced by college professors, but the charter members also were justifiably proud of their principled outlook and progressive ways and wanted those who followed to know about the challenges they faced and overcame.

In March 1907, just two months after the new club had elected its first slate of officers, The Mountaineers put out its first publication, *The Mountaineer*. It was the first of four editions that were later bound together in a single volume as the first *Mountaineer* annual, for the years 1907 and 1908. Editions of the annual were published nearly every year until 1982, when it lapsed during a time of financial uncertainty. It was brought back in 1991 in a volume that covered the eight years from 1983 to 1990, and since then has appeared every other year.

Before the advent of today's glossy mountaineering magazines and before publishers became interested in mountaineering as a publishing genre, these annuals were the official record of exploratory climbing in the Pacific Northwest. Back issues of the annual are continually referred to by writers and researchers looking for information on first ascents and other historical material to enrich their books and articles.

In the first few years of the club, penny postcards were sent to members listing club meetings and events. In April 1911, The Mountaineers began a monthly bulletin devoted to notices of club activities, which it called *The Mountaineer Bulletin*. In January 1921 that name was shortened to *The Mountaineer*—to the consternation of future researchers who would have to sort out the annual from the bulletin of the same name. The bulletin has evolved into a monthly magazine with a circulation of more than fifteen thousand that publicizes the club's activities, as well as conservation alerts and information of general interest to members.

THE FIGHT FOR *FREEDOM*

When Wolf Bauer taught the climbing course in 1935 and 1936, he wasn't about to let his students off easy. Not only did they have to pass a written test that was similar to a college exam, but climbers also were asked to provide written descriptions of the climbing routes they had used. Eventually, a form was issued to standardize route descriptions. From about 1936, these "Climbers' Guides" were copied and made available at nominal cost.

Within a few years, the climbing course, which initially used British mountaineer Geoffrey Winthrop Young's *Mountain Craft* as a text, felt the need for written materials tailored to local mountaineering. Starting in 1938, each climbing course lecturer was asked to prepare his topic in outline form and submit it to the climbing committee for approval. This was mainly an attempt to eliminate overlap or omissions of important material, but the end result was the first book in the nation devoted exclusively to teaching climbing.

In 1939, climbing course outlines were supplied by George MacGowan, O. Phillip Dickert, Jack Hossack, Lloyd Anderson, William Degenhardt, Walter B. Little, T. Davis Castor, Ken and Phyllis Norden, and others, and the first softcover text of these mimeographed pages was published in 1940 as the *Climber's Notebook*. It contained information on how to tie knots, techniques for climbing on rock and snow, orientation, and first aid. Much of it is as useful now as it was a half-century ago, including such admonitions as "look back to the rear occasionally so you will recognize territory on return," and "be as discriminating in your choice of climbing companions on difficult ascents as you are in selecting your outfit."

In 1948, Seattle's Superior Publishing Company bought the trade rights to the *Climber's Notebook* and published a hardcover, typeset volume titled *The Mountaineers Handbook*, using the same text and illustrations. The Mountaineers retained the copyright. By 1954, when the stock of these books had been nearly exhausted, the climbing committee realized that the book was out of date and a complete revision was

necessary. Climbing chairman Maury Muzzy appointed Harvey Manning to revise the book.

Manning, a club member since 1948 and former chairman of the climbing committee, was outgoing, outspoken, talented as a writer, and a natural for the job. In September 1955, he called a meeting of all the former climbing committee chairmen he could locate. This group drew up an outline of the proposed book and recruited writers to prepare drafts.

"The group then gathered to consider the material," Manning says, adding with characteristic humor, "They met on four consecutive nights, and the members who remained by the fourth night became the book editorial committee."

Some of the relationships formed on this committee were to become long-lasting and productive. Nancy Bickford and Tom Miller later married; Harvey Manning and Ira Spring went on to produce many of the books in the *Footsore* and *100 Hikes* series.

The members of this editorial committee wrote and edited chapters, supervised the efforts of others, attended innumerable meetings and, in countless telephone and campfire conversations, decided every detail of the book down to the finest subtleties of mountaineering equipment and technique.

"Over the years, each chapter was completely redrafted as many as seven times," Manning says, "so that the final version might be the work of one person, the style that of another, with large units of content supplied by several others. The editors sought to balance an overall structural uniformity with maximum retention of individual feeling and tone."

Illustrations were supervised by Nancy Bickford after each writer had submitted proposed drawings for his or her chapter. Tom Miller drew stick figures to indicate what was needed

Harvey Manning, who joined the club in 1948, headed the committee that produced Mountaineering: The Freedom of the Hills, *authored the* 100 Hikes *and* Footsore *series with Ira Spring, and along with Tom Miller headed the club's book publication efforts for eighteen years. Harvey and his wife, Betty, are shown here below Canada's Mount Athabaska in 1950. In the 1960s they took over the North Cascades Conservation Council's newsletter and renamed it* The Wild Cascades. *Under their direction it became one of the liveliest conservation publications in the country.* Photo: Tom Miller.

to illustrate specific points. Artist Robert Cram drew the illustrations involving human figures, and Donna Balch did the remainder. In addition, Dee Molenaar contributed drawings. Photographs were assembled by professional photographers Bob and Ira Spring, with scores of Mountaineers submitting photos.

Typing and proofreading were done entirely by volunteers, one of whom was Peggy Eaton (later Peggy Ferber), who responded to a plea in the bulletin for typists.

"I spent many evenings at home turning handwritten into typewritten copy on my dad's old pre-World War I portable balanced on the night stand," she recalls. "Later I got permission from the office manager at work to use my typewriter there when I had everything else caught up.

"Sometimes when it was slow, the other girls would be filing their nails, reading paperback penny dreadfuls or looking out the window, and I would be over in my corner hammering out copy on rock and snow techniques or the best type of rain gear."

Writing the book was one thing, getting it published was another. A book finance committee was appointed, and found there was little club money available to do it. Then a rumor circu-lated that the club's permanent building and improvement fund was about to be used for

In front of the guide house at Paradise on Mount Rainier in 1939: George Mayle,* Dee Molenaar, Ken Spangenberg,* Clark Schurman, and Cornelius "K" Molenaar.* The Molenaar brothers were touring the United States in a 1928 Model A and this was their first meeting with Clark Schurman, chief guide at Mount Rainier from 1939 through 1942. Schurman convinced Ken and Dee to work as climbing guides the next summer, and the Molenaars traded milking cows for climbing expeditions. Dee contributed drawings for the first edition of Mountaineering: The Freedom of the Hills, and his book The Challenge of Rainier was published by The Mountaineers in 1971. Schurman was a leading figure in Northwest mountaineering and scouting, and Camp Schurman, at Steamboat Prow on the east side of Mount Rainier, was named in his memory. Photo: Dee Molenaar collection.

Keith Gunnar, a noted and widely published nature photographer, on the ridge leading to Ruth Mountain in the North Cascades (1960). Photo: Frank Fickeisen.

publishing the book. The estimated cost of the project—twelve thousand dollars for the printing of five thousand copies, plus an additional three thousand dollars for manuscript preparation— roused determined opposition from club members who misunderstood where the money was to come from.

"The editorial committee was so discouraged that there was discussion of splitting off from the club and forming a separate organization to present the climbing course," Manning said.

Before that happened, Paul Wiseman became club president. Wiseman was an economist who had been on the original committee that investigated publishing the book, and he understood exactly what risks were involved. His attitude

was unequivocal. Of course the book was needed, he told the committee, adding, "Of course it will be published by The Mountaineers."

The book finance committee concluded that the best plan was to ask club members to pledge money, which could be secured only by the actual books. If the book effort succeeded, the loans would be returned with interest; if not, lenders would receive the unsold books. The first pledge, for five hundred dollars, was made by a member of the committee at its November 1, 1956, meeting. Others followed, especially after the *Mountaineer* bulletin for December carried a pledge form and a plea for funds. But the total was far short of the need. Then a member sent four thousand dollars in cash, with the stipulation that it be paid ahead of all the pledges.

The book finance committee was succeeded by the book promotion committee, and under chairmen E. Allen Robinson and Warren Wilson it expended great energy in raising capital and in figuring out how to promote, sell, and distribute the book. A final rush for pledges and the cash itself was made in 1959 after the board approved the manuscript. A total of 102 people participated in financing the book.

With the money raised, the next dilemma was a title. There already were a great many books called *Mountaineering,* and something more was needed to make this book distinctive. It was Manning who offered the required cachet with his subtitle *The Freedom of the Hills.*

Mountaineering: The Freedom of the Hills was published in April 1960. Robinson had estimated that five thousand copies would last climbing course members for five years. But the book was a hit outside the club as well, and the entire run sold out the first year. By early fall, enough money had been raised from sales to repay every loan in full. What had started out as an in-house endeavor to support the climbing course ballooned into a major publishing event, a testament to the enormous talent and persistence of all those involved.

Freedom entered its sixth edition in 1997 and is regularly used as a textbook by climbing courses around the country. The Los Angeles chapter of the Sierra Club alone has bought several thousand copies at a time for its courses, and the U.S. Army has bought the book for training purposes. Volunteers still do most of the work revising editions of *Freedom,* although for the fifth and sixth editions a professional writer and editor, Mountaineers member Don Graydon, was hired to rework the text.

When the money from the first edition wouldn't stop rolling in, it was decided that a literary fund should be established with an account separate from other club funds to ensure that any money not needed for reprints would be earmarked for further publications. All income from *Freedom* was funnelled into the new fund. The literary fund came about largely for political reasons. Manning and the others who had worked so hard on *Freedom* didn't want to see the fruits of their efforts go to the ski lodges or other club purposes. If they had let the money flood the general fund, The Mountaineers probably would have built more than the four ski lodges that exist today, and there might have been no money to publish other books.

Jesse Epstein, Mountaineers president in 1967–68, drafted a set of regulations for the literary fund to ensure that the fledgling books operation would conform to Internal Revenue Service rules governing nonprofit organizations. The board of trustees established the literary fund committee with the purpose of financing "the publication, from time to time, of such books, pamphlets, or other educational material as shall be authorized and approved by the Board of Trustees in furtherance of the stated purposes of The Mountaineers."

They couldn't have predicted that "from time to time" would eventually come to mean publishing a new book nearly every week of the year.

A BOOK BONANZA

The proceeds from *Freedom* made it possible to publish an English translation of Wastl Mariner's *Mountain Rescue Techniques,* which was so good it was adopted as the preferred text worldwide. Then came several exhibit-format books that had great success in furthering environmental objectives.

The North Cascades was published in 1964,

with text by Harvey Manning and photos by Tom Miller, and was an important instrument in creation of North Cascades National Park. *The Alpine Lakes,* published in 1971 with text by Brock Evans, editing by Manning, and photographs by Ed Cooper and Bob Gunning, is credited with saving the Alpine Lakes Wilderness from a presidential veto. In 1984, *Washington Wilderness: The Unfinished Work,* a book by Manning with photos by Pat O'Hara, helped bring about passage of the Washington State Wilderness Act.

In 1966, *100 Hikes in Western Washington* by Louise Marshall and Ira Spring was published. In following years, other guidebook editions were written by Manning, with photos by Spring. The *100 Hikes* series supplanted *Freedom* as the golden goose, with revenues surpassing all previous books and thus allowing continued growth of the literary fund. Over the years, these guides have developed into a series of books that are credited with introducing more people to the safe and responsible use of the backcountry than perhaps any other Northwest publications. They pioneered the way for numerous similar guides featuring bicycling, kayaking, ski touring, and snowshoeing as well as hiking.

Harvey Manning and Tom Miller were the team that kept the books projects moving along for eighteen years. Manning was the easily ignited spark plug, Miller the calm negotiator who mediated differences of opinion. In addition to contributing photos for *The North Cascades,* Miller worked on the production side designing the *Alpine Lakes* book and working with Cooper and Gunning to contribute the pictures. Miller also worked with Eric Bjornstad and Fred Beckey on the *Guide to Leavenworth Rock Climbing Areas,* and with Beckey on the first of the *Cascade Alpine Guides* that The Mountaineers

published. He also worked with Pat O'Hara on *Washington Wilderness.*

Most decisions in the early days of the literary fund committee were made during monthly meetings conducted in members' living rooms, the manuscripts handed around after having been drawn out of shopping bags. "The meetings were a juggling act of books that should be done, books that were fun to do, and books that were likely to earn back their investment quickly," said John Pollock, who eventually became head of the books operation. "Even with only two or three new titles a year, there were agonizing decisions as to where to use our limited funds."

A bookkeeper kept preparing worst-case cash flow forecasts for the committee, most of which indicated imminent bankruptcy. But the authors, editors, illustrators, and others were almost always so consistently behind schedule that expenses could be postponed, and sales were just enough ahead of forecasts that the bank balance remained positive.

Then came a watershed event for the books operation, one of the first steps in moving from a volunteer club activity to the professional publishing operation of today. In 1976, the club rented a booth at the American Booksellers Association's annual meeting in San Francisco. Donna DeShazo, a climber and then volunteer publicist, and committee chairman Pollock not only brought back thousands of dollars worth of book orders but established contacts with publishers around the world that would lead to co-publishing and other joint ventures.

In 1978, Pollock was offered the job as first paid director for the books operation. This decision represented a major turning point for the club, according to James Sanford, Mountaineers president in 1978–79.

"The change was fundamental," Sanford

Donna DeShazo in front of Dome Peak on a Ptarmigan Traverse outing in 1968. Originally a volunteer, like everyone else in the early days of the club's publishing efforts, DeShazo took on more and more responsibilities and was eventually hired as the director of the Books division. Under her leadership, the division became one of the largest publishers of outdoor books in the country. Photo: Pat Loveland.

wrote in the 1980 annual. "While we had paid for certain club administrative functions for many years, here we were taking a function which had been built and operated solely by volunteers and now were placing it under the management of a paid director."

DeShazo, who joined the staff in 1979, became manager of Mountaineers Books in 1982 after Pollock left, then director in 1985. She held that position until retiring in January 1997. She says of the decision to hire a paid director: "It was time to recognize the growth

of Books. We were running a program with half a million dollars in sales out of people's living rooms."

A paid staff further meant that a permanent office was required. "Books," as it was beginning to be called, wound up in the rear portion of street-level space below the clubrooms. Pollock basically moved in a desk and chair, and that was the office. Nevertheless, it was a real office with regular hours, and authors began to come in with proposals, some of which managed to survive the literary fund committee reviews. The small staff got so used to climber-writers dropping by on their travels that even the neophytes could spot the Himalayan veterans—the ones missing the first joints on some of their fingers.

As the club's book catalog grew from a single-page flyer to several pages of titles, the antics outside the door on Pike Street kept the staff scrambling. Drunks would sometimes collapse in the entryway, and irate customers smashed the windows of the Soft Touch body painting studio across the street. All the while, The Mountaineers kept unloading books from printers' trucks in the alley, which was paved with the green glass of broken wine bottles.

The old building wasn't hazardous, but it could be trying on those who worked there, according to the Books staff. There was the case of The Clicker, as he was dubbed, the phone caller who rang at sometimes five-second intervals for hours at a time, only to hang up when the phone was answered. The phone company was no help, and despair grew.

"Then one morning for some reason I yanked on the phone cable where it came through the wall into my office," DeShazo says, "and discovered that for nearly a foot all the gray plastic covering had been chewed off the bundle of wires and many of the wires themselves had been gnawed by a rat."

A trap was placed in a restroom, and the following Monday morning an anguished cry from the first person through the door announced that the rat responsible for the phantom phone calls had been caught.

THE BECKEY GUIDES

In 1949, when Fred Beckey published his first guide to cliffs and glaciers of the Cascades and Olympics through the American Alpine Club, he helped set off an explosion of interest that

Fred Beckey practices his climbing moves on Monitor Rock (now called Schurman Rock) at Seattle's Camp Long in 1939. Beckey went on to bag hundreds of first ascents, perhaps more than any other climber in the world. Fred wrote the first local mountain guidebook, Climber's Guide to the Cascade and Olympic Mountains, published by the American Alpine Club in 1949. It soon became known as "Beckey's Bible," a name it retains today in its current three-volume incarnation as the Cascade Alpine Guide, now published by The Mountaineers. Photo: Lloyd Anderson.

ultimately made the state's mountain ranges famous. His Climber's Guide to the Cascade and Olympic Mountains of Washington is the prototype upon which many other guides are based. This volume, with 271 pages of detailed route descriptions, plus notes on geology, climate, and natural as well as climbing history, soon became known as "Beckey's Bible." It was as indispensable a rucksack item as a map.

The Mountaineers subsequently published an edited and expanded edition of *Climber's Guide*, which became the *Cascade Alpine Guide* series of three books, and Tom Miller initially worked with Beckey on the new guides.

"Fred is certainly a diligent and dedicated researcher—that's what you hope for in a guidebook author," Miller says. "He tracked down people who had done routes, no matter how obscure or undistinguished. He'd find out what they did and write it all up."

John Pollock tells of spending many long evenings poring over material with Beckey in all-night coffee shops. Beckey would send in parts of the manuscript written on place mats from restaurants across the West, and he would mail committee member Peggy Ferber postcards giving corrections, sometimes for parts of the work he hadn't even sent her yet.

Each Beckey guide would start out as a sheaf of blank paper, each sheet headed with the name of a mountain and perhaps an elevation. Then Beckey started filling in the blanks, Ferber recalls. "I would get letters and postcards from wherever he happened to be, with new information on routes as he explored them or received information from other climbers. Eventually, all the pieces fit. . . ."

Beckey has published other books through The Mountaineers as well, including the *Darrington and Index Rockclimbing Guide*, the *Guide to Leavenworth Rock Climbing Areas* with Eric Bjornstad, *Mount McKinley: Icy Crown of North America*, and the autobiographical *Challenge of the North Cascades*. In addition, The Sierra Club published his exhibit-format book *Mountains of North America*, and Beckey recently finished a study of the earliest history of the Cascade Range.

EXPLORING SUCCESS

An ability to change directions quickly and capitalize on unforeseen opportunities helped make Mountaineers Books a success. In 1976, The Mountaineers published *Fire and Ice* by Stephen L. Harris, a rather scholarly work about the Cascade volcanoes with a cover featuring an aerial close-up of a steam vent on Mount Baker, then the hottest thing in the range. The literary fund had serious reservations that it would ever sell, and it was published only because there seemed to be a need for such a book.

That need was borne out a few years later when Mount St. Helens started shaking. A new edition of the book was rushed into print and had been out only a few weeks when the volcano erupted on May 18, 1980. Mount Baker was bumped off the cover for a photo of St. Helens in full eruption, and orders for *Fire and Ice* poured in from all over the country.

In 1978, the literary fund committee was replaced by two committees, one to critique publication content and one to ensure financial soundness. Finally, the two committees were merged into a books management board.

Since the club left its Pike Street building, the book publishing operation has been housed separately from the other club offices because of the need for warehousing (now some three-quarters of a million individual books) and for a full-fledged shipping and receiving operation. Mountaineers Books is presently located on Harbor Island in a Seattle industrial district, where the staff of some twenty-five people carry out the administrative, editorial, production, marketing, and distribution functions of a trade publishing operation. Production facilities are fully computerized to take advantage of the latest in digital print-production techniques.

The Mountaineers currently publishes approximately forty titles a year, with about four hundred titles in print. The club has become one of the largest publishers of outdoor books in the nation, and the leading English-language publisher of mountaineering titles. In the tradition of *Freedom* and the early local hiking guides that helped build the program, the bulk of the publishing list is still how-to titles on technique and safety in outdoor activities, and where-to guidebooks for exploring everywhere from pockets of backyard wilderness to the barely charted regions of the planet.

Like the activities of the club itself, the scope of Mountaineers Books' publishing list has expanded to include guides to many regions of the country as well as mountainous areas of the world. The club also pioneered family guidebooks to the outdoors with first one, then two, volumes of hikes to take in the Puget Sound region with children. This has expanded to a series of more than twenty-three titles covering areas across the country.

Conservation and environmental issues continue to be a major publishing interest, with such subjects as the western forests, the ancient-forest campaigns, the Pacific fisheries crisis, and the fate of the Columbia River and other Northwest rivers the focus of recent books. In addition, every guidebook published by the club contains extensive material promoting responsible use of outdoor recreation areas.

The club's publishing program has long since included recording the history of mountain exploration through accounts of international expeditions in the Himalayas and other regions, including cooperating with European publishers to generate works by such world-class mountaineers and writers as Eric Shipton, H. W. Tilman, Kurt Diemberger, Chris Bonington, Reinhold Messner, Joe Simpson, Greg Child, David Roberts, and John Roskelley.

Club publications are marketed internationally wherever there is an interest in mountaineering and adventure literature, and translation rights are sold as well. There are Japanese language editions of *Medicine for Mountaineering* and *Hypothermia, Frostbite and Other Cold Injuries,* German- and Italian-language editions of *Freedom,* and a Dutch edition of *Walking Austria,* among many others.

Art Freeman, the current director, was brought on staff in 1982, when Donna DeShazo, early in her tenure, realized that someone with formal training in business administration and financial management would be needed for the enterprise to grow and prosper. According to Freeman, "the success of Mountaineers Books can be attributed to several factors, including DeShazo's strong leadership and the vision and dedication of the many volunteers who laid the foundation for success in the early years and who currently provide support and guidance to the staff. Of no less importance is the organization's commitment to producing books that not only embody the club's mission and values but that also meet the highest quality standards—a commitment that attracts both expert authors and top-quality professional staff."

Considering that all books published must support the stated purposes of the club rather than seek to exploit market opportunities alone, the books operation has achieved an enviable record against strong competition from other publishers who have moved in to serve the outdoor niche. This success has made book publishing an important element in the fiscal health of the club.

Chapter 13

SOMETHING HIDDEN

By 1914 the Mountaineers had their mountain retreat at Snoqualmie Lodge. But it wasn't enough to satisfy the demands of a growing membership, and pressure grew for a home for those who loved the wilderness but were not drawn to climbing or winter sports. This yearning was satisfied in 1915 with acquisition of what came to be known as the Rhododendron Preserve, near Chico in Kitsap County on the western edge of Puget Sound. The unique Forest Theater and Mountaineers Players drama group followed.

By the time of the Kitsap purchase, club members had been taking local walks to the area for several years and were familiar with the mysteries of the old-growth forest there. They had stumbled upon the Hidden Valley ranch of Edward Paschall in 1909, and club members found they shared a deep kinship with Paschall and his family. Morda Slauson reconstructed that initial meeting of minds in the wilderness in the 1956 annual:

"Spring sunshine wove gay patterns through the darkness of the virgin forest. On a narrow deer trail, winding through the trees, were a happy party of sixty-six Mountaineers. They were searching for Wild Cat Lake where, they had been told, a lavish display of native rhododendrons could be seen in full bloom. They also were looking for a lunch stop.

" 'This way,' decided John Best, leader. The party followed him down a sharply dropping hillside. The lake, at last? But no, they stood on the edge of a deep, green valley, as hidden as a bird's nest in a wilderness of towering firs and cedars. There was no sound except the music of two clear streams; no motion save the drift of blue wood smoke from the chimney of a rustic cabin.

"Then the door opened and a man strode out, his hand outstretched in welcome. The warmth of that first handclasp has lasted forty-seven years.

"Thus The Mountaineers in 1909 made the acquaintance of Edward Paschall and Hidden Ranch. Within a matter of minutes they had met his wife and two of his daughters, Mary and Patience, for their host turned and went back to the cabin, saying firmly, 'Come out and meet these nice people.' "

Among the "nice people" in that Mountaineers group were some of the best-known club members at the time, including John A. Best Jr., Lydia E. Lovering, Nancy Emerson Jones, Cora Smith Eaton, and Mabel "Fuz" Furry. This was a highly literate bunch, and Paschall might have mentioned that what had inspired him to leave the small town in Pennsylvania where he had been editor of a country newspaper and head west in 1907 was a poem, Rudyard Kipling's "The Explorer":

> "Something hidden—go and find it!
> Go and look behind the ranges!
> Something lost behind the ranges—
> Lost and waiting for you.
> Go!"

The Mountaineers' own philosophy was reflected in those lines, and club members shared with the Paschall family a love of learning as well as a love for the wilderness. This close affinity lasted throughout the lives of all involved. Edward, Mary, and Patience Paschall joined The Mountaineers, and Mary later married another Mountaineers member, William Remey. Patience lived the rest of her life at Hidden Valley and frequently participated in club events.

The Mountaineers soon adopted Hidden Valley as their own.

"Following that first spring walk, rhododendron sightseeing trips became an annual event," Slauson continued in her 1956 account. "Later, salmon walks were added in the fall when the great fish came up the creeks to spawn. As many as 225 people would take the little steamer *Norwood* at Galbraith dock in Seattle and chug across Puget Sound to Chico. Once off the boat, they'd shoulder packs and climb the old hill trail, past the dripping ferny clay banks and marshy Tame Cat Lake to the first Mountaineers shelter. This was an

S. Edward Paschall became fast friends with club members and worked with them over the years to preserve the spectacular forest surrounding Hidden Valley Ranch. The club established what may be the first true forest theater in the country on property adjacent to Paschall's. Photo: Celia D. Shelton, Special Collections, University of Washington Libraries, neg. no. 18144.

abandoned log cabin that became temporary headquarters for overnight parties."

The Mountaineers had found their own bit of paradise, but they had no illusions that it would remain as it was without a struggle. The ancient trees were being cut down all around Puget Sound, and the property adjacent to Hidden Valley had fallen into the hands of a timber company. Therefore, in 1915, through the combined efforts of Edward Paschall and Peter McGregor, seventy-four acres of hill land adjoining Hidden Ranch were purchased by The Mountaineers.

In 1918, McGregor told of negotiations stretching out over years. The timber company

had taken the land for a bad debt and held it at
a value of $1,800 to $2,000. Through a series of
complex negotiations in which McGregor took
the initiative, The Mountaineers finally bought
it for $371.

An additional thirty acres was purchased in
1917, but the legal documents to both properties were in such a mess that gaining clear title
proved a monumental task requiring eighteen
years of paperwork. The job of writing letters
wasn't finished until September 1935, when
ownership to all 104 acres was finally settled in
favor of The Mountaineers.

The Kitsap purchase wasn't without contro-
versy in the club. Some members questioned
whether it was a wise decision. In the 1916 annual, Mary Paschall was foremost in its defense:
"The query as to the purpose of the Kitsap
property is perhaps partially answered by the
use which has been made of it since May 6,
when it was first opened. Of the 409 members
and guests who registered in the six months,
223 are included in the annual rhododendron
walk. The remainder came in small parties. The
Kitsap preserve is a park in the larger sense, and
as such will have more significance as time
passes. It may well be styled the kindergarten of
the club as the beautiful Snoqualmie Lodge in
its mountain environs is the finishing school.

"In these lower playgrounds lies everybody's
chance to become a pioneer in woodcraft, to
learn to make a fire in a rainstorm, to follow the
unmapped forest with only his compass, to read
the writing on the trail. When he knows his forest as the seaman knows his sea, he is prepared
in a peculiar sense to go forth alone and un-
afraid in answer to the trumpets of the winds
that are ever calling man up into the high
mountains."

The Paschalls helped The Mountaineers buy
additional acreage in the years that followed,

✧

*Peter McGregor, a leader and pacemaker on
numerous outings, is shown with his famous whistle
on the summit of Glacier Peak during the 1921
outing. McGregor, a charter member, helped secure
the Rhododendron Preserve property, using his own
money to make the down payment, and worked
tirelessly for years to gain clear title to the land. His
pail of lemonade with its ring of tin cups was a
familiar campfire feature on the outings, as he'd
circulate with the pail, bringing refreshment to the
tired trekkers.* Photo: P. M. McGregor, Special
Collections, University of Washington
Libraries, neg. no. 18118.

and the daughters donated part of their property to the club in the 1950s. In addition, The Mountaineers Foundation will inherit Hidden Valley itself under terms of a bequest by Patience Paschall.

Mary Paschall Remey and Patience Paschall summed up Mountaineers feelings in 1955 when they made a gift of additional property: "Down through the years these forest ways have felt the feet of many lovers of wilderness; artists finding peace and strength from the big trees, botanists searching for fungi, ferns or orchids, poets caught in the spell of the lavish rhododendrons, or the lone fisherman splashing softly through the unending loveliness of an April river. There are no words to capture values such as these."

KITSAP CABIN

By 1917, Mountaineers were dreaming of a new cabin to replace the crumbling two-story log house that was on the Kitsap property when they bought it. "The dream is as yet unrealized, but the hope of its fulfillment makes the problems of decaying timbers and sagging corners of the present log house, of wells which are empty, or else too much inhabited, and how to build a $75 fireplace for $25 seem mere trifles. And when they get too difficult—the problems—we go down to Hidden Ranch and listen to 'Fiddle and I' and forget our troubles," Arthur Loveless wrote in the 1917 annual.

The new Kitsap Cabin, built during World War I in a mere six months, stands as a monument to Harry Myers and Otto Voll and their crew of volunteer women. Since the war had taken most of the men away, it was the women who split the shakes, nailed them on, and lugged stones for the chimney. Mary Paschall was especially prominent among them.

The cabin was built at a cost of six hundred

Mabel "Fuz" Furry, shown during the 1920 outing to the Olympics, was among the "nice people" who stumbled across the Paschall ranch in 1909. Known for her photos and sketches, she attended at least thirty-six summer outings between 1911 and 1952 and was devoted to the Rhododendron Preserve and Forest Theater. Photo: Special Collections, University of Washington Libraries, neg. no. 18149.

dollars, compared with an estimated twenty-five hundred dollars had hired labor and purchased materials been used. The relative thrift was due in part to C. G. "Gus" Morrison, a contractor who helped the club secure the best building materials at the lowest cost. Morrison would do the same for the new Snoqualmie Lodge thirty years later.

On November 23, 1918, Kitsap Cabin was dedicated, club president Edmond Meany presiding. The cabin was a small wooden structure consisting of a common area and a kitchen, but it was home to many members on weekends.

At the time, it was Mountaineers policy to allow members to purchase strips of land in or adjacent to the Rhododendron Preserve. They could then build their own cabins or lean-tos, and many of the cabins on the property originated in this way. This idea was probably the brainchild of Edward Paschall, who was unable to bear the thought that the huge Douglas firs on the hillside above Lost Creek might someday disappear. He therefore bought a forty-acre tract encompassing the largest trees and sold ribbon strips of three acres each to Mountaineers members, who agreed to preserve the beauty of the Puget Sound forest in their individual plots. Each strip started at the foot of the hill in Lost Creek and progressed up the wooded slope to the dense rhododendron thickets on top.

As time passed, it became evident that this plan was impractical. Loggers constantly sought to buy the strips away from the families that owned them, and those trees standing at the edges of the strips were saved several times only by the fast efforts of Patience Paschall and Mary Paschall Remey. Finally, the owners concluded that the strips could best be preserved by adding them to the rest of The Mountaineers' property. In 1957, after a few had been donated to the club, most of the strips were repurchased, with the last one being donated to the club in 1989.

The driveway leading to Kitsap Cabin was part of the original Chico Trail, also known as Kitsap County Road 289. When the county planned the current highway in 1923, it intended to follow the designated road, but this would have put Kitsap Cabin on one side of the road and the Forest Theater on the other, so the county agreed to move the highway to the north of the cabin. The effect was to divide the property into a fifty-three-acre theater and cabin tract and a northwest portion of about fifty-two acres.

MOUNTAINEER PLAYERS

There's strange things done
'Neath the Kitsap sun
And stranger things yet
In the rain.
—Morris Moen, 1984, "Elegy for Harriet King Walker, 1893–1984"

Early pantomimes and plays at the Rhododendron Preserve were done solely for the entertainment of fellow Mountaineers and for the satisfaction that artistic self-expression provided. However, as early as 1926, strangers were noted in the audience. No special effort was made to attract the public, but in the early 1930s it became apparent that more people outside the club were coming to the productions, and so they were formally opened to the public. On several occasions over the years, the theater has squeezed 1,450 people onto the hillside, and today audiences of 600 to 900 are not uncommon.

It all goes back to the first theatrical efforts at the preserve. Among the first that had any real continuity occurred on Halloween night 1917 in front of the old log house on the property when the headless rider of Sleepy Hollow fame was acted in pantomime.

"This stunt was acted on a bright moonlit Halloween night. The actors wore sheets, rode sticks with carved horses' heads and tore around at terrific speed," according to Katha Miller-Winder, historian for the Mountaineers Players, the club's drama group. "The climax was reached when one of the ghosts took off his head, a football, and threw it into the midst of the audience assembled around the campfire."

The next spring, a few excerpts from *Robin Hood* were acted in appropriate spots in the forest below Hidden Ranch. The audience followed the actors through the trees for the production, most of it more or less impromptu. Joe Hazard was Little John, and he and Harold

Sexsmith fought "a most exciting duel on a tree trunk that had fallen across the creek."

With the completion of Kitsap Cabin in 1918, these little productions became increasingly sophisticated.

"During the year, the cozy interior of the new cabin has been the background for several high-class vaudeville performances, merry dances and community sings, and the open fireplace has been the social center for many 'a feast of reason and flow of the soul,'" the 1919 annual reported.

One of the cleverest stunts of the time was the christening of Mary Paschall's cow, done with all the form and solemnity of a High Anglican service. It was apparently a regular occurrence, as the cow is recorded as having been christened

A favorite skit at Hidden Ranch was the christening of Mary Paschall's cow. Repeated many times, it had all the trappings of a High Anglican service. Such skits became more and more elaborate until they evolved into the Players group. Photo: Mabel Furry, The Mountaineer annual, 1918.

The May Queen and "her" retinue of "ladies-in-waiting" celebrate May Day in 1918. The queen was played by tough-guy climb leader L. A. Nelson, while the "ladies" included Harry Myers and Peter McGregor. Photo: Fairman B. Lee, Special Collections, University of Washington Libraries, neg. no. 18145.

Guiding Star, Genevieve, and Liberty Bell, among other names. The skit was complete with choir, soloist, and someone to officiate. The various roles were assigned to whoever was handy. A note in the Mountaineer Players historian's files indicates that for the May Day fete in 1918, during the parade to Hidden Ranch for the christening of the cow, Harry Myers and Peter McGregor were the ladies-in-waiting, while Mr. L. A. Nelson took the part of the May Queen.

The first true play occurred on June 17, 1923, when the group presented the ambitious musical pantomime *Robin of Sherwood*, based on a poem by Alfred Noyes. This time there was a stage manager, costumes rented from Roosevelt High School in Seattle, singers of ability, music from violin and cornet, and a background of folk dancing. This play was done so beautifully that the Mountaineers took to dramatics in earnest and started in a businesslike way to obtain professional training. Under the direction of

Mabel Furry, they formed a drama class and placed themselves under the instruction of drama coach Lois Sandall.

Next came another pantomime, *The Shepherd in the Distance*, by Holland Hudson, on May 25, 1924. Then, on June 7, 1925, the first vocal production debuted: *The Little Clay Cart*, a Hindu drama ascribed to King Sundrake in about A.D. 400, with the cast composed entirely of Mountaineers women.

By 1925, it was evident that better theater accommodations would have to be found, especially for the mosquito-tortured audiences that now numbered over two hundred at each performance. The audience had to stand or sit on the ground, which was always wet, and in addition the original theater site was not on Mountaineers property. Will Darling scouted around for a better "stage" and came up with a level place that had a sloping hill where the audience could sit and look down on the players. This is claimed to be the first true forest theater in the West.

"There are other outdoor theaters, to be sure, but none quite like ours, none that seems to have grown up out of the ground as a very part of the virgin forest. For its wings, five or six on a side, tall enough to conceal the actors, were made of upright slabs of cedar bark. The logs cut in clearing the hillside were piled at the back of the stage and covered with earth and banked with ferns to form an upper level. A huge log was maneuvered into place to mark the front of the stage, and though it has now returned to dust, the great sword ferns set along it still take the place of footlights. Green mosses were draped over the wings and huge ferns set in every corner and cranny—all to blend with the verdant forest background," Harriet K. Walker noted in the 1956 annual.

The new theater was dedicated on June 6,

1926, by Edmond Meany, followed by the play *Reginald and the Red Wolf*. The theatrical climax of those early days was reached on June 5, 1927, when *Alice in Wonderland* was produced. This was such a success that the Seattle Chamber of Commerce asked The Mountaineers to reprise it for convention-goers in Seattle.

What began as a single annual performance blossomed into a run of eight performances per year. Only the director, music director, accompanist, and sometimes choreographer have ever received any payment. Everything else is done by volunteers, including in 1958 when railroad track was laid for the production of *Annie, Get Your Gun*. Since the theater has no curtain, the railroad coach was rolled onto the stage with the actors on it. For the 1987 *Robin Hood—The Musical*, the Players dug a pond on the stage, and during the quarterstaff fight between Robin and Little John, both actors were knocked into the water. The dirt floor of the theater soaked up the splashes.

The size and nature of the Forest Theater stage allow for sets that create actual places. The village in *Donegal Fair* in 1959, for example, was built with a thatched roof made by tying bundles of straw to chicken wire. The rainy weather helped make the roof look authentic.

The Players have tried to remain faithful to their commitment to retaining a true forest theater, while making modifications necessary to modern life. They now use a few strategically placed microphones to compete with the occasional noise of aircraft passing overhead, and rely on an electric piano that remains in tune despite many moves and changes in the weather.

Over the years the Players have been remarkably fortunate with the weather. For the first thirteen years, the rains held off. But in 1935, with the production of *Toad of Toad Hall*, it

Harriet Walker was best known for her participation in the Players, appearing in thirty-eight of their productions and writing two of them, Ali Baba and the Forty Thieves *(1932 and 1940) and* Under Richard's Banner *(1936). She also took part in sixteen summer outings and climbed, hiked, and skied with the Club.* Photo: Mabel Furry, Harriet Walker Album, The Mountaineers Archives.

rained so hard that the jaws of the toad mask became glued together and the actor had to shout through a soggy mess. Despite the rain, the audience refused ticket refunds and the show continued.

In recent years, preservation of the Forest Theater can be credited to the perseverance and dedication of one man, Gardner Hicks, and his committee. Hicks took over the job of theater maintenance in 1970 and has been at it ever since.

A PRICELESS LEGACY

Now things are rather different from the early days of Kitsap Cabin. No longer does C. M. Bixby haul supplies purchased at his little store in Chico to the cabin in his horse-drawn wagon, along with the members' camping equipment brought over on the steamer *Reeve*. Supplies are brought in from Seattle or purchased in Silverdale. With the advent of the highway, few hike to the property anymore, preferring to drive and save their legs for a trek to Big Tree or some other popular destination.

From the original 74 acres of land in 1915, the preserve has grown to more than 240 acres. Through the years, additional parcels have been obtained for the Rhododendron Preserve by purchase and donations. One of these was paid for by concerned club members when the opportunity to purchase arose but The Mountaineers did not have the funds. These individuals contributed a thousand dollars each, purchasing a parcel of about eight acres east of the Forest Theater from the estate of William Wymer.

The property adjoining the theater, about fifty acres, had been offered to the club by Wymer, but the negotiations were too slow and he sold the tract instead for logging. As a result, trees belonging to The Mountaineers were cut, and the club sued Wymer to collect damages. About eight hundred dollars was received, which resulted in Wymer harboring less than cordial feelings toward The Mountaineers. He subsequently sold off other parcels at the present entry to the property, and sometime around 1960 put a chain across the entrance road one Saturday just before a play was due to open. It required a judge's order to force him to remove it.

The Mountaineers sued to establish its right of access across Wymer's property, and the case went all the way to the state Supreme Court. The club was victorious due to the fact that both the Paschalls and The Mountaineers had used the road for at least thirty years. Up to that time, the club believed it owned the road.

In 1982, William Wymer's son, Bill Wymer, sought to sell ten acres for fifty thousand dollars. The Mountaineers didn't have the money, but gathered contributions totaling fourteen thousand dollars, which Wymer accepted for the five acres along the east border of the preserve. He stated that it was worth something to him to have his property bordered by people who would preserve it. In 1997 The Mountaineers Foundation purchased the remaining property owned by the Wymer family along the eastern border of the preserve, thus ensuring that no residential development will take place near the Forest Theater.

Although The Mountaineers Foundation, formed in 1968, is a separate entity from The Mountaineers, it shares a close relationship at the Rhododendron Preserve through a conservancy agreement and a management agreement.

In 1983 a federal law was passed allowing certain types of nonprofit organizations to put qualifying property into conservancy status, relieving them of the burden of most property taxes. It was decided this should be done with most of the Rhododendron Preserve. In 1985

The Players have tried to remain faithful to the spirit of a true forest theater, but a few modifications have been made to deal with modern life. For example, hidden microphones help actors be heard over the sound of passing aircraft. This scene is from the Players' 1942 production of "The Princess and Mrs. Parker." About all that has changed since then is that the trees have grown larger. Photo: Georgia Graham, The Mountaineer annual, 1977.

the club transferred all but twenty acres to the foundation, since The Mountaineers itself does not meet the legal requirements necessary to place property in conservancy status. The transfer was due in large part to the efforts of Morris Moen, a past president of both the club and the foundation and an active Mountaineers Player. The twenty acres retained by The Mountaineers contain the Forest Theater and Kitsap Cabin, structures that made those portions of the land ineligible for conservancy.

The preserve remains a wilderness habitat of great scientific interest and beauty. Streams crossing the property host several species of salmon, which spawn from late August until early fall. Their skeletons can be found on the banks under the alders and maples until spring, when small animals chew them up for the calcium they provide. Above the streams are old-growth fir, cedar, hemlock, and pine. The old-growth trees range in age from one hundred to four hundred years.

Salmonberry, salal, Oregon grape, sword fern, devil's club, huckleberry, and rhododendron carpet the forest floor, often to a depth of six feet or more. The rhododendrons are everywhere, ranging in size from twigs to giants twenty feet high. One area contains stands of pine resistant to blister rust, which has destroyed many of the pine trees in the Puget Sound region. It is not known why these trees have survived while others have not, but it is important to preserve them for study.

The Mountaineers Foundation's Kitsap holdings—some of the last remaining virgin lowland forest in the Puget Sound region—are designated among the state's Natural Heritage Lands.

THE TRAIL AHEAD

Reflecting on the history of The Mountaineers, it's surprising to note how much has remained consistent over nearly a century. On any given weekend, men and women can still be found leaving the city under the guidance of fellow club members to climb and ski and hike. There remains a general disregard for the trappings of social status and financial success. One still earns the respect of fellow members by being a safe and competent climber, hiker, or kayaker, not by wearing the flashiest gear.

The lure of "freedom of the hills," an appreciation for adventure, and a conservation-oriented respect for the beauty of the natural world still bring people together under the club's umbrella, just as in 1907. The adventures are perhaps more thoroughly pre-explored these days, and modern gear may provide a slight edge, but basic activities are much the same. In nearly one hundred years, the club's purposes have been amended only once, and that to broaden the scope of the organization beyond the confines of the Pacific Northwest.

Even with this continuity, the club faces significant challenges as it heads into the twenty-first century. A second and third generation of conservation activists must now deal with backlashes from commercial and industrial interests, as well as increased factionalism among the many conservation organizations. And the threats to preserving the natural beauty of the Pacific Northwest and beyond continue unabated. Truly sustainable forestry remains an unattained goal. While The Mountaineers helped create numerous parks and wilderness areas, only vigilance will ensure their preservation. Funding for maintenance of national parks and wilderness areas has steadily declined, and trails have deteriorated. The concept of user fees for access to these areas has gained acceptance.

Early in the club's history, members were aware of the potential degradation of the wilderness by forestry, agriculture, and industry. Only in the past twenty years, however, has overuse by eager and occasionally ignorant hikers and climbers also become a threat. Management agencies often see restrictions on recreational use as the easiest way to counter the problem. Thus, responsible access to the backcountry—the kind of access needed by a wilderness activities club—is no longer assured.

The gnarly dilemma of loving the wilderness to death has brought a reexamination of club practices and a newfound appreciation for "leave no trace" ethics. Increasingly the club finds itself negotiating carefully with land managers to assure them that the club supports and understands their difficulties while at the same time protecting the right of responsible access to the wilderness without unreasonable and bureaucratic restrictions.

Guidebook author and Mountaineers member Ira Spring notes that the "Forest Service policy of ensuring solitude for hikers is going to have a tremendous impact." He said that proposals to reduce weekend use in the Alpine Lakes Wilderness by 68 percent and in the Gifford Pinchot National Forest by 50 percent will make it necessary for permits to be requested well in advance of a trip, long before trail and weather conditions can be known.

The Mountaineers club has always been active in building and maintaining trails for access to peaks and the backcountry. In recent years, emphasis has shifted to saving existing trails. Ira Spring says hundreds of trails have been saved because they were featured in Mountaineers guidebooks. "At first, trails were lost primarily due to road building by the logging industry," he said. "Now the main danger is neglect."

Mountaineers Books faces many challenges as it strives to educate and inspire the outdoor community through quality publications. Demographics and the tastes of book buyers are always shifting and must be anticipated. The Internet, CD-ROM, and other yet-to-be imagined technologies may radically change the way publishers deliver their goods to consumers. In addition, the marketplace is increasingly crowded with newcomers eager to take advantage of the growing interest in outdoor books. While these newcomers have had varying degrees of success, none of them to date has displayed the adherence to mission, principles, and quality that has set Mountaineers Books apart from the crowd for so long.

Finally, club leaders rightly must question how the organization might make the best use of the Books division in fulfilling the overall club mission. With money in the bank, The Mountaineers is in the enviable but surprisingly difficult position of determining how to best allocate resources for the good of the whole. Thus, a major question for the future is how much should be devoted to further publishing efforts as opposed to dozens of other competing opportunities, including programs for environmental education, conservation, and access, to name just a few.

Maintaining the spirit of volunteerism that is a hallmark of the club is another challenge of the new century. It seems that as the pace of life has increased, the availability of a large volunteer pool is no longer assured. Building a lodge using only volunteers as workers is now hard to comprehend. Even so, a recent survey showed that one out of five members had served as a volunteer with the club in the previous year.

Also affecting the volunteer nature of the club is the membership growth over the past ten years. At fifteen thousand members, the club is not as "clubby" as it was. Systems and customs that served a smaller club are strained by the need to assimilate new members at a faster rate while at the same time nurturing new volunteer leaders for outings and club management.

Another issue is the growth of the club's branch organizations. In a larger club, the relationship of the branches to the "nonbranch," or Seattle-based club, becomes more problematic. How much control should the main club have? What does it mean to be a branch? How much autonomy should the branches have? The larger question here concerns club governance in general. The board of trustees has often struggled to find the right administrative structure to serve members. It's an ever-shifting concern that becomes even more important as the club grows.

In fact, as this book goes to press, president Bill Maxwell is leading the board in a thorough review of the club's mission and values and the role of the board as a policy-making and governance (as opposed to management) body, with one important goal of determining the best organizational structure to carry The Mountaineers into the next millennium. Once this review is accomplished the search to fill the executive director slot vacated by Suzanne Weckerly in March 1998 will begin.

The size of the club, both in members and assets, has brought changes that require a more business-like approach: formal personnel systems, high-tech methods of communication, sophisticated marketing techniques for books, and the like. But at the same time that staff employees handle more of the technical side of running the club, volunteers and all other members stand, as always, at the heart of the organization as the ones who give it life and purpose.

Longtime club president Edmond Meany summed up The Mountaineers' mission in the 1910 annual: "This is a new country. It abounds in a fabulous wealth of scenic beauty. It is possible to so conserve parts of that wealth that it may be enjoyed by countless generations through the centuries to come. . . . This club is vigilant for wise conservation and it is also anxious to blaze ways into the hills that anyone may follow."

Meany's faith in the effectiveness of dedicated environmentalism has inspired generations of club members to do their part for wise conservation. But even Meany could hardly have foreseen the numbers of people who now seek relaxation, and spiritual and physical renewal, in exploring this new country, where the "fabulous wealth of scenic beauty" now risks serious depreciation.

Potential conflicts over the right of access to the wilderness and the need for conservation face not only The Mountaineers but every lover of the outdoors. On this and other issues of concern to the outdoor community, The Mountaineers will continue to be a leader in both philosophy and action.

Ruth Ittner (left) and Sam Fry (right) were instrumental in creating Washington State's SnoPark program in the mid-1970s and the Iron Goat Trail project (in partnership with Mount Baker–Snoqualmie National Forest) in the 1990s. Fry is a past president and climbing chairman of the club, was in charge of the third edition of Mountaineering: The Freedom of the Hills, *and received the Service Award in 1986. He helped organize Volunteers for Outdoor Washington (VOW) in the early 1980s. Ittner has also been a tireless worker with VOW and numerous other outdoor volunteer and trails efforts. In 1998 she received the American Hiking Society's prestigious Jim Kearn Award. She has been the club's Trails Coordinator since 1975 and in 1987 received the Service Award. Photo: Sam Fry*

The committee that planned the 1925 outing to the Snoqualmie Pass–Teanaway area included Glen
Bremerman, Ben Mooers, Matha Irick, and Charles Farrer. Farrer joined the club in 1907 and was still
attending summer outings in 1959 at the age of ninety-three. Born in Massachusetts and educated at Eton in
England, he migrated to Colorado, where he worked as a cowboy, ranch foreman, and stagecoach driver. He
then headed to Alaska and the Klondike to prospect for gold before settling in Seattle in 1905, where he
worked for the Humane Society, eventually becoming its president. Photo: P. M. McGregor, Special
Collections, University of Washington Libraries, neg. no. 18125.

Left: Margaret Hazard and Ben Mooers show off the latest styles in climbing clothes during the 1923 outing
to Mount Garibaldi in British Columbia. This was the first outing outside the United States, and the first on
which the dress code was relaxed and women were permitted to wear pants or bloomers before reaching camp.
"Hazzie," a Mountaineer from 1912 until her death in 1979, served many years on the board, on most of
the club's committees, and was editor of the Bulletin. Together with her husband, Joe, she was a strong
advocate of wilderness protection. Mooers was also a longtime member and an outing and club leader.
Photo: P. M. McGregor, Special Collections, University of Washington Libraries, neg. no. 18136.

Dee Molenaar and Pete Schoening tend to blisters and bruises near the Fisher Chimneys following a 1991 climb of Mount Shuksan. (They were accompanied by Austrians Fritz Wintersteller and Marcus Schmuck, who made the first ascent of Broad Peak in the Karakoram Range in 1957.) Photo: Pete Schoening collection.

Right: By 1940, access to the Olympic Mountains was easy compared to what it had been thirty years earlier. All one had to do was drive to the trailhead. Sitting on a pile of gear at the start of the 1940 summer outing to the Olympics: Linda Coleman, Crissie Cameron, Florence Dodge, and Hannah Bonnell, all longtime outing participants. Photo: Mabel Furry, Special Collections, University of Washington Libraries, neg. no. 18152.

Above: The scouts for the 1924 outing to Mount Rainier included, from left, Clarence "Happy" Fisher, Harry Rowntree, Paul Hugdahl, Amos Hand, and Lars Lovseth. Fisher and Hand continued to be outing and climb leaders for many years, and Lovseth was one of the early skiing pioneers. Photo: P. M. McGregor, Special Collections, University of Washington Libraries, neg. no. 18151.

On the way to Diamond Head in Garibaldi Provincial Park, British Columbia, in 1958: Stella Degenhardt, Bob Sexauer, Vin "Cal" Magnussen, Hal Williams, and Dick Curran. Photo: Frank Fickeisen.

Charles Albertson, shown on the summit of Mount Hood during the 1911 outing, was a powerhouse climber who set an example that other club members would strive for decades to match.
Photo: Charles Albertson Album, The Mountaineers Archives.

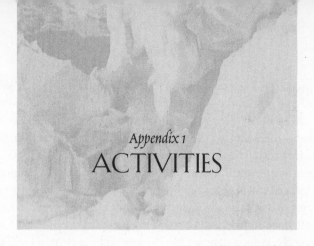

The list of club-sponsored activities has changed constantly in the years since The Mountaineers was founded in 1906. Activities have come and gone, depending on the interests and dedication of the volunteers who run the committees. Once-popular groups such as Summer Outings and Campcrafters (car camping) have vanished, but other groups have taken their place. Still other activities have continued as a close part of the club since its earliest days, such as climbing, photography, and nature study.

Here are brief descriptions and histories of some Mountaineers activities:

Alpine Scrambling: In the late 1960s the climbing committee decided to organize a new course that would alleviate overbooking of the basic climbing course. The idea was to offer something less technical that would appeal to people who sought wilderness travel and mountain climbing, but not necessarily the rigors and dangers of roped climbing. The scrambling course offers just about everything taught in the climbing course, including ice-ax techniques, but does not include roped climbing.

Backcountry Skiing: This program teaches telemark turns, winter travel on cross-country skis, and ski mountaineering to those who want to traverse the backcountry during snow season.

Backpacking: Mountaineers climbing parties that stayed out overnight with their Trapper Nelson packs, relying on such foods as rice, flour, beans, cheese, and crackers, inadvertently pioneered backpacking. But the backpacking program didn't officially begin until 1970, when the first trips appeared in the bulletin under their own heading. Backpacking trips are now rated from easy to very strenuous, with hikes suitable for all ages and strength levels.

Bicycling: Most Mountaineers riders are experienced adults with road bikes, but the program offers a variety of rides throughout the year, including mountain biking. During the summer, longer outings are offered, while winter brings seminars on bicycle care and repair.

Climbing: Techniques are constantly being evaluated and revised for use in the basic and intermediate courses. Climbing program innovations supplement the content of *Mountaineering: The Freedom of the Hills*, now in its sixth edition. Instruction has been expanded to emphasize low-impact wilderness travel and leave-no-trace camping, and a conservation service requirement is now part of the basic course.

Comrades: Formed in 1993 with the name Not So Fleet of Foot, the Comrades offers a year-round agenda of hikes, rock climbs, skiing, snowshoeing, scrambles, and backpacking—but at a relatively slow pace. The more challenging activities require graduation from the appropriate course.

Dance: The Saturday night dance is a long-time Mountaineers institution. Some of the earliest dances began during the Depression, when cheap entertainment was in short supply. Contra dancing, country and western, swing, and ballroom dancing all have enjoyed renewed popularity. More recently, zydeco dancing has been added to the mix.

Family Activities: In spring 1976, a group called Campcrafters was formed as an offshoot of the backpack committee, with events geared toward families and children. The current family activities program serves as the successor to Campcrafters. Its most popular trips involve car camping, but weekends at the lodges also get a good turnout.

First Aid: Mountaineering oriented first aid (MOFA) focuses on illness prevention and accident response in the wilderness. The first-aid committee recruits and trains instructors, in cooperation with the American Red Cross, who provide courses for an average of five hundred students a year. The MOFA course is nationally recognized, and the club's textbook, *Mountaineering First Aid*, has been updated through four editions since it was first published in 1972. The *MOFA Instructor Manual*, also published by The Mountaineers, is in its second edition.

Foreign Outings: The foreign outings program, established in 1973, sponsors foreign travel in an atmosphere of goodwill and respect for other cultures.

Hikes: Hikes are offered year-round, ranging from easy to long and very strenuous. Trips to foreign locales have become popular, including places in England, France, Austria, and Australia. Summer outings in the early days of the club included hikes in which sixty or more people took part, and even as late as the 1970s, a total of thirty or forty hikers was common. Safety and environmental concerns finally led to a limitation, beginning in the 1980s, of twelve in a party.

International Exchange: The International Exchange was formed as a way of sharing mountaineering skills and environmental philosophies with people from other countries, and to extend the purposes of The Mountaineers to the world at large. As one example, in 1995 Mountaineers hiked in Italy as guests of the Pisa section of the Italian Alpine Club, and in 1996 The Mountaineers hosted members of the Pisa section on Northwest climbs and treks.

Junior Mountaineers: Young people are involved in a wide array of Mountaineers programs. The youth committee sponsors snowshoe trips, lodge trips, and outreach activities; the conservation education program seeks volunteers for the Conservation for Kids program in public schools; and The Mountaineers Foundation has joined with the Sierra Club to sponsor a youth leadership training program.

Kayaking: Wolf Bauer, the climber and skier who helped start the climbing course in the mid-1930s, also was a kayaker and introduced the sport to club members after World War II. This early group was not formally a part of The Mountaineers, but most of its members were Mountaineers. The Mountaineers offered its first organized paddling activity in 1986, and now gives courses in both sea kayaking and white-water kayaking.

Naturalists: The study of nature was a key interest of the club's founding members. A botany group, or "botany bunch," was organized not long after the club was formed in 1906. In 1972, finding the word "botany" too restrictive, members changed the name to Naturalists.

Photography: The photography program offers outings, seminars, a nature photography course, exhibitions, competitions, and support for conservation activities. Photo subjects during excursions range from ocean to mountains, vegetation to wildlife, forest to urban jungle. Mountaineers photographers have been published in books including *Washington Wildlife Viewing Guide,* Nature Conservancy publications, and magazines including *Cascade Crest* and *Outdoor & Travel Photography,* as well as Mountaineers publications.

Retired Rovers: Since this group was formed in 1979, its brown-bag lunch meetings at the clubhouse on the second Tuesday of each month have grown to include more than a hundred people. Retired Rovers sponsors activities geared for retirees, including hikes and backpack trips, bicycle rides, winter snow excursions, and trips to Mexico, Canada, and Japan.

Sailing: The sailing program offers a crewing course to train club members to sail on boats owned by experienced Mountaineers skippers. The course focuses on the basics of crewing rather than on boat handling, which can be taught by the skippers on a one-to-one basis. Program members donate the use of their own boats because they like teaching, gain needed crew members, and enjoy socializing with like-minded sailors.

Singles: This program initially was controversial because it was based on a status rather than on a specific activity. But its popularity won out, and in 1997 it was one of the club's fastest-growing groups. In fact, any club member—single or not—is eligible to participate in the activities, which include hiking, bicycling, skiing, snowshoeing, sleigh rides, tennis, volleyball, dancing, plays, concerts, photography, book discussions, game nights, and potlucks and other social gatherings. For outdoor trips, training and equipment requirements are consistent with other Mountaineers standards.

Snowshoeing: In the early days, snowshoeing was not viewed as a separate activity but simply as a means of getting into the mountains in winter. Once the snowshoers reached their destination, perhaps Snoqualmie Lodge or Paradise at Mount Rainier, winter games including snowshoe races were the order of the day. In the early 1960s, snowshoe trips were sponsored by Viewfinders, the precursor to the scrambling program. In 1965 snowshoeing became a separate activity with a committee of its own.

Trails: This program promotes the preservation and inventorying of Washington trails and helps land management agencies review their policies and regulations. It also teaches hikers how to care for the trails they use.

Appendix 2
MOUNTAINEERS PRESIDENTS

Henry Landes, 1907–08
Edmond S. Meany, 1908–35
Elvin P. Carney, 1935–37
Hollis R. Farwell, 1937–38
Harry L. Jensen, 1938– 40
George MacGowan, 1940– 42
Arthur R. Winder, 1942– 44
Burge B. Bickford, 1944– 46
Lloyd Anderson, 1946– 48
Joseph Buswell, 1948–50
T. Davis Castor, 1950–52
William A. Degenhardt, 1952–54
Chester L. Powell, 1954–56
Paul W. Wiseman, 1956–58
John R. Hazle, 1958– 60
E. Allen Robinson, 1960– 61
Robert N. Latz, 1961– 63
Frank Fickeisen, 1963– 65

Morris Moen, 1965– 67
Jesse Epstein, 1967– 68
John M. Davis, 1968– 69
Max Hollenbeck, 1969–71
James Henriot, 1971–73
Sam Fry, 1973–75
Norman L. Winn, 1975–77
James S. Sanford, 1977–79
A. J. Culver, 1979–81
Errol Nelson, 1981–84
Delmar Fadden, 1984–86
William Maxwell, 1986–88
Carsten Lien, 1988–90
Dianne Hoff, 1990–92
Don Heck, 1992–94
Craig Rowley, 1994–96
Marcia Hanson, 1996–98
William Maxwell, 1998–2000

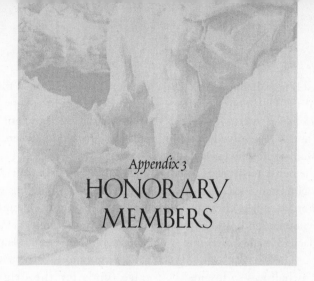

Appendix 3
HONORARY MEMBERS

In 1909 The Mountaineers began bestowing the title of honorary member on individuals who had made notable contributions to climbing, to preserving the wilderness, or to the club itself. Honorary members range from a Supreme Court justice to a woman who began her twenty years of conservation work at the age of sixty-seven to the first American to climb Mount Everest. The reasons for bestowing honorary memberships have been equally varied, and provide insight into club philosophies. Many of those who received the distinction were regular members of The Mountaineers, while others were not affiliated with the club. Following is a roster of honorary members, and brief profiles of each one.

E. S. Ingraham, 1909
S. Edward Paschall, 1921
J. B. Flett, 1922
S. Hall Young, 1926
William B. Greeley, 1929
Mary E. Wright, 1936
A. H. Denman, 1938
H. B. Hinman, 1940
Charles Albertson, 1940
O. A. Tomlinson, 1942
Charles M. Farrer, 1944
Peter M. McGregor, 1946
Clark E. Schurman, 1950
John Osseward, 1954
W. Montelius Price, 1960
Leo Gallagher, 1960
Edward W. Allen, 1961

Howard Zahniser, 1962
Wolf Bauer, 1966
William O. Douglas, 1967
David R. Brower, 1967
Patrick Goldsworthy, 1969
Emily Haig, 1972
Bradford Washburn, 1973
Terris Moore, 1979
Jesse Epstein, 1988
James W. Whittaker, 1990
Fred W. Beckey, 1992
Maynard Miller, 1993
Dee Molenaar, 1993
Polly Dyer, 1994
Pete Schoening, 1996
Ira Spring, 1997

1909. Major Edward Sturgis Ingraham, a charter member, moved to Washington territory from Maine in 1875 at age twenty-three, became an explorer, and was involved in early climbs of Mount Rainier. Ingraham was the source of many of the best-known place names in Mount Rainier National Park, including Camp Muir (site of an overnight encampment with John Muir), Summerland, and Elysian Fields. Ingraham Glacier is named after him.

1921. S. Edward Paschall was so inspired by Rudyard Kipling's poem "The Explorer" that he left Pennsylvania and his life as editor of a country newspaper to head West. His quest led him to Hidden Valley near Chico on the western shore of Puget Sound in 1907. He helped The Mountaineers acquire the adjoining property, which became the Kitsap Rhododendron Preserve, and fought numerous early environmental battles alongside the club.

1922. John B. Flett was a charter member and one of the great early Northwest climbers. He led the first ascent of Little Tahoma, in 1894, and was among the group that claimed the first ascent of Mount Olympus, in 1907. He eventually became a National Park Service ranger, and after retiring devoted himself to the club's Rhododendron Preserve.

1926. Samuel Hall Young, a Presbyterian minister known as the "mushing parson" for his dogsled travel in Alaska in the late nineteenth century, accompanied John Muir on his explorations of Alaska's Glacier Bay area and was himself an explorer and naturalist.

1929. William B. Greeley was chief of the U.S. Forest Service from 1920 until 1928. Greeley

promoted the concept of the tree farm, and as Forest Service chief apparently was sufficiently aware of the environment that he drew the praise of The Mountaineers.

1936. Mary Estelle Wright was a charter member who, with her husband, Seattle lawyer George E. Wright, championed many environmental causes. She had a hand in efforts to build a climbers hut at Camp Muir on Mount Rainier, promote construction of trails, and raise funds for the original Snoqualmie Lodge.

1938. Asahel Holmes Denman was largely responsible for the formation of the Tacoma branch of The Mountaineers, in 1912. Under his leadership, the branch pioneered winter outings to Mount Rainier and thereby led the way to winter sports in the Northwest. Denman Peak and Denman Falls in Mount Rainier National Park are named for him.

1940. Harry B. Hinman established the first Mountaineers branch, in Everett in 1910. At the time, there was no provision in the bylaws to allow a branch, but due to Hinman's efforts the club's constitution was changed to allow them. Mount Hinman in the Cascades is named for him.

1940. Charles Albertson was one of the most active and powerful climbers in the Pacific Northwest in the early days of the club. He attended his first summer outing in 1909, during which he climbed Mount Rainier with the first large party to ascend by way of Camp Curtis.

1942. Owen A. Tomlinson, superintendent of Mount Rainier National Park in the 1920s and

1930s, often allied with The Mountaineers in its conservation battles. Club members and Tomlinson worked together in 1928 to defeat a proposal to build a tramway from the snout of the Nisqually Glacier to the upper bluffs of Paradise Valley.

1944. Charles M. Farrer joined The Mountaineers in 1907 and was club secretary during the critical period of 1908–14. He was still attending summer outings in 1959, at age ninety-three.

1946. Peter M. McGregor was a charter member, an unofficial member of the first six summer outing committees, and on the board of trustees for more than fifteen years. He served as club treasurer and chairman for local walks, and was instrumental in helping secure the Kitsap Rhododendron Preserve.

1950. Clark E. Schurman joined The Mountaineers in 1936. He was chief guide at Mount Rainier from 1939 through 1942, and after his wife died he devoted his energies to Scouting and to developing mountaineering techniques and a safety-oriented climbing philosophy. Mount Rainier's Camp Schurman is named after him.

1954. John Osseward set the pattern of factual presentation that was to become a hallmark of effective environmentalism. During World War II, the timber industry wanted to cut lowland forests in Olympic National Park on the pretense that Sitka spruce was needed for manufacturing airplanes. Osseward's arsenal of facts demolished industry arguments at a hearing before U.S. Representative Henry Jackson of Washington State.

1960. W. Montelius Price was the charter member who first discussed formation of a Seattle mountaineering club with Asahel Curtis during the 1906 Mazamas outing to Mount Baker. He is credited along with Curtis with the first ascent of Mount Shuksan, in 1906, and was on the first ascent of Mount Olympus with The Mountaineers in 1907.

1960. Leo Gallagher joined The Mountaineers in 1919 and devoted himself to the club. He was chairman of the Tacoma branch, chairman of Tacoma's Irish Cabin, and headed the club's summer outings on three occasions. In addition, he was a pioneer in nearly every major conservation effort of the time.

1961. Edward W. Allen joined The Mountaineers in 1910 and was a key figure in getting Moran State Park established on Orcas Island. In 1920, as secretary of the state Board of Park Commissioners, he was able to push through acceptance of the deed to the property over the objections of Governor Louis Hart. Allen's action revived interest in state parks, which had been languishing for years.

1962. Howard Zahniser, who was executive secretary of The Wilderness Society, is considered the "father of the Wilderness Act." Zahniser established the concept and design of the National Wilderness Act of 1964 and was noted for encouraging organizations such as The Mountaineers to pursue their own goals in establishing wilderness areas.

1966. Wolf Bauer joined The Mountaineers as a Boy Scout member in 1929 and taught the first climbing course in 1935. Bauer made significant contributions in every area of his expertise:

mountaineering, skiing, mountain rescue, kayaking, and conservation engineering.

1967. William O. Douglas championed many environmental causes as a U.S. Supreme Court justice. In August 1958, when The Mountaineers and Olympic Park Associates were fighting an effort to build a road along the Olympic National Park ocean wilderness strip from the Hoh River to Cape Alava, Douglas led some seventy hikers down twenty-two miles of beach to protest the action. The road was never built.

1967. David R. Brower has been a major figure in the conservation and environmental movement for more than forty years. As the first executive director of the Sierra Club, he brought the organization back to the passion of its most prominent founding member, John Muir. He joined The Mountaineers in 1960.

1969. Patrick Goldsworthy became a Mountaineers member in 1953 and quickly became involved in environmental activism, particularly the establishment of North Cascades National Park. In 1969, the director of the National Park Service appointed Goldsworthy the sole citizen member of the North Cascades National Park master plan team, which planned the park and the Ross Lake and Lake Chelan National Recreation Areas.

1972. Emily Haig joined The Mountaineers in 1958 at age sixty-seven, and for the next twenty years left her mark in the conservation field. She was a founding member of the North Cascades Conservation Council and served on the board of trustees for Olympic Park Associates.

1973. Bradford Washburn headed the National Geographic expedition to explore and map the St. Elias Range in Alaska, but he is best known in mountaineering circles for his exploits on Mount McKinley. He was on the first ascent of McKinley's West Buttress route, in 1951, and his magnificent photos of the mountain drew climbers from all over the world to McKinley.

1979. Terris Moore was a pioneer in mountaineering, credited with first ascents of Minya Konka on the Chinese–Tibetan border, Sangay in Ecuador, and Bona, Fairweather, and Sanford Peaks in Alaska.

1988. Jesse Epstein joined the club in 1958 and became one of the most creative leaders in the history of The Mountaineers. He served on ten major committees from 1958 through 1967, and as club president in 1968, was primarily responsible for reorganizing its financial structure. He was the guiding spirit behind The Mountaineers Foundation and also helped establish the literary fund, which led to the club's book-publishing program.

1990. James W. Whittaker joined The Mountaineers in 1944. In 1963 he became the first American to climb Mount Everest. He pioneered the use of climbing to promote world peace, organizing and leading the 1990 Mount Everest Peace Climb in which rope teams that included one American, one Russian, and one Chinese successfully reached the summit.

1992. Fred W. Beckey, a living legend among Northwest mountaineers, is a climber, naturalist, historian, and author. As of 1997, Beckey's astonishingly prolific climbing career had spanned fifty-eight years. Beckey dropped out of The Mountaineers in 1989 over dissatisfaction with the club, but later accepted honorary membership, renewing his association with the organization that had been a part of his early climbing adventures. Beckey has amassed more first ascents than perhaps anyone else on earth, ranging from the North Cascades to the Himalayas.

1993. Maynard Miller, who joined The Mountaineers in Tacoma in 1938, has been on expeditions ranging from Bradford Washburn's 1940 venture to the Fairweather Range of Southeast Alaska to glacier and geological studies in the Himalayas. His principal focus over the past fifty years has been the relationship between worldwide climatic trends and glaciers.

1993. Dee Molenaar, who became a Mountaineers member in 1942, has climbed in the United States, Canada, Europe, New Zealand, Antarctica, and the Himalayas. His book *The Challenge of Rainier,* published by The Mountaineers in 1971, is the definitive work on the mountain's history.

1994. Polly Dyer has been one of the most influential environmentalists in Washington State for more than forty years. Dyer, who joined The Mountaineers in 1950, led the fight in the 1970s to add Shi Shi Beach and Point of the Arches to Olympic National Park, as well as the successful effort to prevent a proposed highway along the wilderness coast.

1996. Pete Schoening became a member of The Mountaineers in 1947. In 1958 he and Andy Kauffman achieved the first ascent of Hidden Peak in the Karakoram Range—becoming the only Americans ever to make the first ascent of an 8,000-meter mountain. In May 1996, at age sixty-nine, he attempted to become the oldest person to ever climb Mount Everest, but failed to adapt to the altitude.

1997. Ira Spring joined The Mountaineers in 1941. His wilderness photographs have influenced thousands of people to enjoy and respect the environment. He is co-author of the *100 Hikes* and *Footsore* series of guidebooks, which for more than three decades have introduced people to the glories of backcountry travel in the Northwest.

SOURCES

In this list of sources *The Mountaineer* always refers to the *Mountaineer* annual rather than the monthly bulletin.

CHAPTER 1

Lynch, Frank. Interview with W. Montelius Price. *Seattle Post-Intelligencer*, March 23, 1955.

Warren, Dr. James. History of Edmond Meany. *Seattle Post-Intelligencer*, February 7, 1984.

The Mountaineer 1 (1907–08); 30 (1937); 50 (1956).

CHAPTER 2

The Mountaineer 1 (1907–08); 2 (1909); 3 (1910); 5 (1912); 30 (1937); 50 (1956).

CHAPTER 3

Winn, Karyl. Interview with Herman Ulrichs, 1973 (University of Washington Special Collections).

The Mountaineer 6 (1913); 7 (1914); 12 (1919); 15 (1922); 16 (1923); 18 (1925); 25 (1932); 26 (1933); 27 (1934).

CHAPTER 4

The Mountaineer 28 (1935); 29 (1936); 30 (1937); 31 (1938); 32 (1939); 34 (1941); 36 (1943); 38 (1945); 39, no. 14 (1948); 40 (1949); 45 (1952); 46 (1953); 48 (1955); 50 (1956); 51 (1958); 53 (1960); 56 (1963); 57 (1964); 72 (1977); 74 (1980).

CHAPTER 5

Johnston, Greg. "History of Silver Skis competition." *Seattle Post-Intelligencer*, April 18, 1994.

Kjeldsen, Jim. Interview with Wolf Bauer. October 23, 1995.

Rayl, Jo A. Interview with Irene Meulemans and Stella Degenhardt. November 1996.

The Mountaineer 5 (1912); 9 (1916); 13 (1920); 15 (1922); 20 (1927); 21 (1928); 25 (1932); 26 (1933); 28 (1935); 29 (1936); 32 (1939); 39, No. 13 (1947); 39, No. 14 (1948); 50 (1956); 56 (1963).

CHAPTER 6

Mountaineer Bulletin, June 1946 and December 1960 (The Mountaineers Library).

The Mountaineer 21 (1928); 22 (1929); 23 (1930); 32 (1939); 37 (1944); 38 (1945); 39, No. 1 (1946); 39, No. 14 (1948); 40 (1949); 50 (1956).

CHAPTER 7

Kjeldsen, Jim. Interview with Wolf Bauer. October 23, 1995.

Potterfield, Peter. *In the Zone: Epic Survival Stories from the Mountaineering World* (Seattle: The Mountaineers, 1996).

Mountaineer Bulletin, June 1948 (The Mountaineers Library).

The Mountaineer 32 (1939); 39, No. 14 (1948); 40 (1949); 42 (1950); 47 (1954).

Mountain Rescue Council Newsletter, No. 133 (April 1989).

"Wolf Bauer, Otto Trott, Ome Daiber: Best of buddies founded the Mountain Rescue Council." *Seattle Post-Intelligencer*, February 12, 1993.

CHAPTER 8

Kjeldsen, Jim. Interview with Lloyd and Mary Anderson. October 25, 1995.

Kjeldsen, Jim. Interview with Jim Whittaker. November 10, 1995.

Manning, Harvey. *REI: 50 Years of Climbing Together* (Seattle: Recreational Equipment Inc., 1988).

CHAPTER 9

Avery, Mary W. *Washington: A History of the Evergreen State* (Seattle: University of Washington Press, 1965).

Cutright, Paul Russell. *Theodore Roosevelt: The Making of a Conservationist* (Urbana: University of Illinois Press, 1985).

Dryden, Cecil. *Dryden's History of Washington* (Portland, Oregon: Binfords & Mort Publishers, 1968).

Lien, Carsten. *Olympic Battleground: The Power Politics of Timber Preservation* (San Francisco: Sierra Club Books, 1991).

Marsh, Kevin R. "From Conservation to Environmentalism: The Evolution of Three Major Alpine Clubs of the Pacific Coast." Seminar paper, June 1988 (Mountaineers Conservation Division archives).

Zalesky, Philip "The North Shore of Lake Quinault: A Tribute to Polly Dyer." *Voice of the Wild Olympics* (newsletter of the Olympic Park Associates), January 1994.

Zalesky, Philip. Interview with Brock Adams, 1993.

Zalesky, Philip. Interview with Edward Allen, 1965.

The Mountaineer 1 (1907–08); 2 (1909); 5 (1912); 7 (1914); 42 (1950).

CHAPTER 10

The Mountaineer 10 (1917); 23 (1930); 35 (1942).

The Seattle Weekly, Sepember 28, 1983.

Personal recollections of John Davis, Paul Wiseman, Frank Fickeisen, and others.

CHAPTER 11

The Mountaineer 2 (1909); 3 (1910) 5 (1912); 6 (1913); 50 (1956).

Personal recollections of Philip Zalesky (Everett branch), Alice Bond (Tacoma branch), and Paul Wiseman (Olympia branch).

CHAPTER 12

The history of the Books Division was researched by Donna DeShazo, former director of the division, based on documents in division files, interviews with participants, and personal recollections.

CHAPTER 13

The Mountaineer 8 (1915); 9 (1916); 10 (1917); 11 (1918); 12 (1919); 16 (1923); 17 (1924); 18 (1925); 19 (1926); 50 (1956); 51 (1958); 52 (1959).

History of the Mountaineers Players and the Rhododendron Preserve was researched by Katha Miller-Winder based on division files and personal interviews with participants.

INDEX

Boldface numbers refer to photo captions

THE MOUNTAINEERS, founded in 1906, is a nonprofit outdoor activity and conservation club, whose mission is "to explore, study, preserve, and enjoy the natural beauty of the outdoors. . . ." Based in Seattle, Washington, the club is now the third-largest such organization in the United States, with 15,000 members and five branches throughout Washington State.

The Mountaineers sponsors both classes and year-round outdoor activities in the Pacific Northwest, which include hiking, mountain climbing, ski-touring, snowshoeing, bicycling, camping, kayaking and canoeing, nature study, sailing, and adventure travel. The club's conservation division supports environmental causes through educational activities, sponsoring legislation, and presenting informational programs. All club activities are led by skilled, experienced volunteers, who are dedicated to promoting safe and responsible enjoyment and preservation of the outdoors.

If you would like to participate in these organized outdoor activities or the club's programs, consider a membership in The Mountaineers. For information and an application, write or call The Mountaineers, Club Headquarters, 300 Third Avenue West, Seattle, Washington 98119; (206) 284-6310.

The Mountaineers Books, an active, nonprofit publishing program of the club, produces guidebooks, instructional texts, historical works, natural history guides, and works on environmental conservation. All books produced by The Mountaineers are aimed at fulfilling the club's mission.

Send or call for our catalog of more than 300 outdoor titles:

The Mountaineers Books
1001 SW Klickitat Way, Suite 201
Seattle, WA 98134
1-800-553-4453
e-mail: mbooks@mountaineers.org
website: www.mountaineers.org

Other titles you may enjoy from The Mountaineers:

100 CLASSIC HIKES IN WASHINGTON
Ira Spring & Harvey Manning
A full-color guide to Washington's finest trails by the respected authors of more than thirty Washington guides, written with a conservation ethic and a sense of humor, and featuring the best hikes in the state.

MOUNTAINEERING: The Freedom of the Hills, Sixth Edition
Don Graydon & Kurt Hanson
Revised and expanded edition of the classic text on climbing and mountaineering techniques, the best-selling mountaineering book of all time.

BEST HIKES WITH CHILDREN, IN WESTERN WASHINGTON AND THE CASCADES, VOL. 1, Second Edition
Joan Burton
A thoroughly revised edition of the best-selling book in the *Best Hikes with Children* series, with approximately twenty new hikes appropriate for families, seniors, and anyone who enjoys an easy dayhike.

HIKING THE GREAT NORTHWEST: The 55 Greatest Trails in Washington, Oregon, Idaho, Montana, Wyoming, British Columbia, Canadian Rockies, and Northern California, Second Edition
Ira Spring, Harvey Manning, & Vicky Spring
The latest edition of this classic hiking guide to the most spectacular trails in the region, featuring new color photos and the personal picks of a trail-tested team of Northwest hiking gurus.

OUTDOOR LEADERSHIP: Technique, Common Sense & Self-Confidence
John Graham
The best handbook available on outdoor leadership, covering skills applicable to all endeavors and vocations.

SOUVENIRS FROM HIGH PLACES: A History of Mountaineering Photography
Joe Bensen
A stunning survey of climbing imagery over the last 150 years, spanning early landscape paintings to today's award-winning photos, and capturing the development of mountaineering from the distinctive viewpoint of the participants.

TREE HUGGERS: Victory, Defeat, and Renewal in the Northwest Ancient Forest Campaign
Kathie Durbin
A timely account of the high-profile campaign to preserve the Northwest's ancient forests, chronicling twenty years of the battle over old-growth logging with an insider's point of view.

AN ICE AXE, A CAMERA, AND A JAR OF PEANUT BUTTER: A Photographer's Autobiography
Ira Spring
The beautifully illustrated autobiography of a Pacific Northwest hiking, climbing, and skiing guru—an influential trails advocate and the successful photographer and author of more than sixty works.